ART
DECO

ART DECO

The Twentieth Century's Iconic Decorative Style, from
Paris, London, and Brussels to New York, Sydney, and Santa Monica

ARNOLD SCHWARTZMAN

RIZZOLI
NEW YORK

New York · Paris · London · Milan

Front cover:
Entrance Hall,
Eltham Palace, 1936.
Eltham, Greenwich, UK.
Architects:
Seely and Paget.
Designer: Rolf Engströmer.

Back cover:
Metal frame,
The Daily Telegraph
newspaper building, 1928.
(Now Goldman Sachs
International).
135-141 Fleet Street,
London, EC4.
Architects:
Elcock and Sutcliffe
with Thomas Tait.

Endpapers:
"Speed of Transportation",
Port-cochère ceiling fresco.
Artist: Herman Sachs.
Bullocks Wilshire
department store, 1929.

Half Title page:
Statue of Atlas.
Sculptor: Lee Lawrie.
Rockefeller Center,
Fifth Avenue, NYC, USA.

Title page:
Detail,
decorative mural,
map of the North Atlantic.
Dining Room,
RMS Queen Mary, 1934.
1126 Queens Highway,
Long Beach, CA, USA.
Artist: MacDonald Gill.

Opposite:
Bronze directory board,
Los Angeles Times.
Times/Mirror Building,
1931-35.
First and S. Spring Street,
Los Angeles, CA, USA.
Architect:
Gordon Kaufmann.

Overleaf:
Granite relief,
entrance to
Banco Hispano-Americano.
Now Mandarin Hotel.
Passeig de Gràcia 38-40, Barce-
lona, Spain.
Architect:
Manuel Ignacio Galíndez.
Sculptor: Frederic Marès.

Dedicated to my wife, Isolde, whose art production skills
have magically brought the images in this book to life.

First published in the United States of America in 2019 by
Rizzoli International Publications, Inc.
300 Park Avenue South
New York, NY 10010
www.rizzoliusa.com

Originally published in the United Kingdom in 2018 by
Palazzo Editions

© 2018 Palazzo Editions Ltd.

Design, text, and photographs copyright © 2018 Arnold Schwartzman
Design by Arnold Schwartzman
Art Production by Isolde Schwartzman

2019 2020 2021 2022 / 10 9 8 7 6 5 4 3 2 1

ISBN: 978-0-8478-6610-6

Library of Congress Control Number: 2018947039

Printed in China

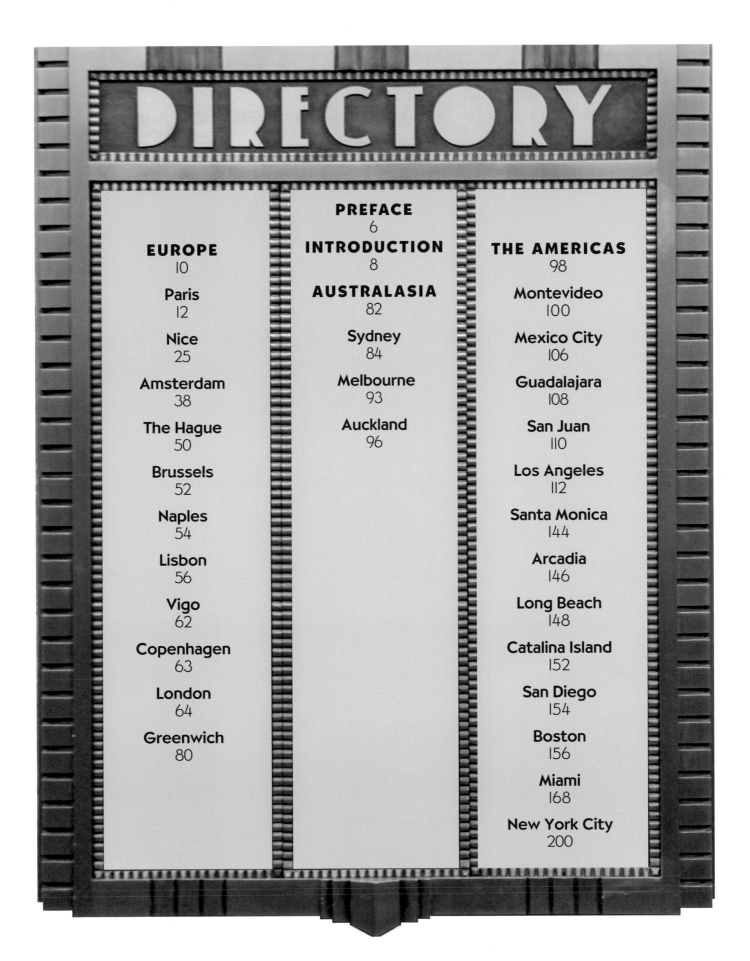

DIRECTORY

PREFACE

As the song goes: "Trains and boats and planes are passing by They mean a trip to Paris or Rome…"

Shortly after the end of WWII, at age eleven, I made my very first venture abroad to spend my school holidays with my great aunt and uncle in Paris.

My British passport, signed by His Majesty's Principal Secretary of State, Ernest Bevin, commanded that I "pass freely without let or hindrance".

When Bevin was asked by a journalist what his foreign policy was, he replied: "To be able to take a ticket at Victoria Station and go anywhere I damn well please".

On my arrival by ferry at Calais, I boarded the plush Deco interiors of the Pullman Flèche d'Dor (The Golden Arrow) boat train that sped me to Paris, "The City of Light", where I first became enamored with the city's architectural beauty.

Speaking to legendary film director Michael Powell some time ago, I asked Michael why he and his partner Emeric Pressburger chose a target as the symbol for their film production company, "The Archers". He explained that they found a James Agate verse to be a perfect metaphor for hitting their target of perfection:

The arrow was pure gold
But somehow missed the target.
Still, as some Golden Arrow trippers know,
'tis better to miss Naples than hit Margate.

My post war Margate home was nestled adjacent to the 1930s Moderne-designed Palm Bay Estate. I recall that one of the home owners had painted Tudor beams over the white stucco facade of his house, obviously not a fan of the Moderne style!

As a documentary filmmaker, and as an occasional on board cruise ship lecturer, I have had the good fortune to travel extensively with my trusty camera.

From my large collection of photographs taken throughout the years, first on film, and later digitally, I have selected images from the continents of Europe, Australasia, and The Americas, as examples that I feel best demonstrate the essence of Art Deco.

So please allow me to take you on a magical flight of fancy as I retrace my past sixty years of photography, and share the finer details of what I consider to be among the world's most beautiful Art Deco buildings.

INTRODUCTION

" ... A new style will assert itself" — LE CORBUSIER, 1924

Commemorative stamp, Paris Exposition Internationale des Arts Decoratifs et Industriels Modernes, 1925. Design: Robert Bonfils.

The term Art Deco was first coined by Bevis Hillier in his 1968 book "Art Deco of the 20s and 30s", a practical distillation of the title of the 1925 Paris Exposition Internationale des Arts Décoratifs et Industriels Modernes. The Exposition brought the style to the world's attention, its proliferation spreading throughout the four corners of the globe.

Art Deco's influence spread rapidly to New York City, and even to the far reaches of the globe, from Buenos Aires to Shanghai and Bombay, which is believed to possess the world's second largest examples of Art Deco architecture.

The style influenced everything from transportation to fashion, jewelry, furniture, and last but not least, architecture. New materials came into play, such as plastics, chrome, Vitrolite glass and lacquer. Popular motifs abounded, such as fountains and waterfalls, flora and fauna, lightning bolts, plus Ziggurats and Zodiacs.

The new look did not appear out of a vacuum as there were numerous influences which included early precursors such as Mayan, Aztec, Chinese, and Byzantine architecture.

There were several significant design movements in the 19th and 20th centuries, including the Arts & Crafts Movement, 1890-1905, with pioneers such as Great Britain's William Morris, Augustus Pugin and Charles Rennie Mackintosh, and in the United States, architects and designers Green & Green, Frank Lloyd-Wright and Louis Comfort Tiffany.

The enormous interest following British archaeologist and Egyptologist Howard Carter's excavation of Tutankhamun's tomb in 1922 lead to a proliferation of Egyptian revival architecture, particularly in cinemas, of which there were over a dozen throughout the United States alone. In my book "London Art Deco", examples include the Carlton Cinema, Islington and Carrera's "Black Cat" cigarette factory, Camden.

Major exponents of the Art Nouveau style were Hector Guimard in France and Victor Horta in Belgium. In Germany the 1914 Werkbund Exhibition introduced its own expression of Art Nouveau known as Jugendstil. The Vienna Secession creators were the Wiener Werkstätte group of designers and architects like Otto Wagner, Josef Hoffmann, and artist Gustav Klimt. Russian Constructivism pioneers were Vladimir Tatlin, and Sergei Diaghilev's groundbreaking Ballets Russes.

In 1920s Weimar Germany, architect Walter Gropius, the founder of the Bauhaus School, along with Ludwig Mies van der Rohe, were regarded as the pioneering masters of modernist architecture.

In the Netherlands, there was Michel de Klerk's Amsterdam School of Architecture, 1910–30s, followed by De Stijl. As well as architect van Doesburg, the group's principal members were the painters Piet Mondrian, Vilmos Huszár, and Bart van der Leck, plus architects Gerrit Rietveld, Robert van't Hoff, and J.J.P. Oud.

Other influences came into play including Cubism, Surrealism, Futurism, Constructivism, and Dadaism. Oscar Wilde opined that "fashion is a form of ugliness so intolerable that we have to alter it every six months".

Out of this melting pot of styles emerged the new aesthetic of Art Deco, which reached its zenith in 1936, the year of my birth. That year, Great Britain's "RMS Queen Mary" sailed on her maiden voyage and captured the "Blue Ribbon" for her speed crossing of the Atlantic, and Germany launched the Hindenburg airship, both of their interiors are prime examples of the Art Deco style.

In the late 1930s my father was a waiter at London's famed Savoy Hotel. In 1929 the hotel and its adjoining Savoy Theatre, its decor designed by Basil Ionides, embraced the new Art Deco look, as did the sleek ebony cat, "Kaspar", the hotel's mascot. As a child, I was privileged to stroke the cat on my visits to the hotel—today I virtually purr at the sheer memory!

These visits to the hotel resulted in my early exposure to the style. Across the road from the Savoy was architect Oliver Bernard's 1930 Strand Palace Hotel with its magnificent Art Deco lobby, where I was dazzled by the illuminated fluted columns and the octagonal mirrors. As I climbed the plush carpeted stairs, its frosted glass banisters would glow in my face.

My father admired all things Streamlined, which included his chrome-plated 1927 Rolls Shaver with its Greek meander-patterned box, a feature much adopted in the architecture of the period. Today, I cherish my late father's mementos, including his copy of the iconic 1930 Art Deco "Savoy Cocktail Book", in which I loved to trace Gilbert Rumbold's colorful illustrations—my pencil indentations still remain in its pages to this day.

Another of my precious keepsakes is my father's 1936 autograph book. Among its signatures are those of the creators of two of that year's filmatic landmarks of the "Machine Age", Charlie Chaplin's "Modern Times" and H.G. Wells', "Things to Come". My 1936 set of "World of Tomorrow" cigarette cards pay homage to Wells' vision of things to come.

Among the many other personalities whose signatures grace this autograph book, are Walt Disney, Marlene Dietrich, Edward G Robinson, and Loretta Young, whose on-screen persona was considered to be the very essence of Art Deco. Without a doubt my father's stories of serving these personalities influenced my desire to make my future pilgrimage to work in the dream factories of Hollywood.

The 1930s were known as the "Jazz Age", as well as being dubbed "the age of transportation", speed being of the essence.

A request from the Cunard shipping line to display a number of my photographs on their new Art Deco themed MS Queen Elizabeth cruise ship, led to the invitation for me to design two murals for the ship's Grand Lobby. One of the murals, "The Golden Age of Transportation", includes R.J. Mitchell's 1931 Schneider Trophy-winning Supermarine S6B seaplane, the Union Pacific's 1934 City of Salina M-10000 streamlined train, and the Hindenburg airship. The images of trains, boats, and planes rendered in stone, mosaic, and glass have become ubiquitous.

— Arnold Schwartzman, Hollywood, 2018

EUROPE

I have had the pleasure of visiting and photographing much of the Art Deco architecture of the continent of Europe on numerous occasions, Paris being one of the most celebrated exponents of the style.

The city is noted for its grand department stores such as Galeries Lafayette, Au Printemps, Le Bon Marché, and La Samaritaine, all providing heavenly light onto the shoppers from their beautiful Art Nouveau-leaded glass skylights. In 1933, the La Samaritaine store underwent structural changes by architect Henri Sauvage, adding Art Deco elements to its existing architecture.

As my first visit to Paris took place shortly after WWII, at a time when heavy currency restrictions were enforced, evidence of this can be seen by the endorsement stamps in my passport by the Bureaus de Change of Galeries Lafayette and Au Printemps.

From the first floor of the Eiffel Tower I enjoyed the vista of the city before me. Across the bridge below I could see the Palais de Chaillot, built in the Moderne style for the 1937 World's Fair.

On visiting the Palais I was impressed by the amount of singular sculptural pieces and bas-reliefs. Among them are eight gilded female statues flanking either side of the building's vast tiled concourse.

As a teenager I was taken to the Folies Bergère, where with the exception of seeing those poorly clad statues, I blushed at the sight of my very first exposure to female nudity!

The Folies Art Deco facade, designed in 1929 by Maurice Picaud (Pico), had fallen into serious neglect, but thankfully it has recently been restored with glittering gold leaf.

One can find an endless variety of Art Deco-designed wrought iron doors at many of the palatial residences throughout the city. Art Deco butcher shops abound with lush marble facades sporting a variety of Deco lettering styles. Viewing so many stunning examples of the city's Art Deco delights assured me that "We'll Always Have Paris".

On our family's winter breaks, my father would drive us to the South of France, to stay in Nice or Cannes. I found that the Mediterranean style of architecture differs to that of Paris, reflecting the warmth of the Mediterranean sun. This aspect is very much evidenced in their style of architecture, such as the Palais de la Mediterranee, which displays giant bas-reliefs on each of its two towers. One exception is the all-brick Nice Thiers Post Office, so reminiscent of the style of the Amsterdam School of Architecture.

This is a perfect segue to introduce Amsterdam. Among the city's most spectacular buildings is the Hijman Louis de Jong's designed Tuschinski Theatre, which is not typical of the Amsterdam School of Architecture, but is a blend of Art Nouveau, Amsterdam School, and Art Deco forms.

Following the destruction of our home during the London Blitz, I was evacuated to the countryside for the duration of the war. During that time, many of London's ancient and modern buildings were destroyed. I did not return to my place of birth until my return in the 1950s from military service in South Korea, to thankfully discover that many prime examples of Art Deco architecture had survived. I have since lovingly documented these in my book "London Art Deco" (Palazzo Editions).

Among my favorite buildings are the former Daily Express building, the Hoover Factory, Derry & Toms and Barkers department stores, plus the Savoy Hotel and its adjoining theatre.

A unique building is the Tudor-period Eltham Palace, Greenwich, the one-time home of King Henry VIII. In the 1930s, industrialist Stephen Courtauld and his wife Virginia purchased the Palace, transforming its interior into a glorious example of the Art Deco style.

Brussels is mostly noted for its Art Nouveau architecture, but also has some fine examples of Art Deco. Lisbon, known for its Romanesque, Gothic, Renaissance, and Baroque architecture, has a few outstanding examples of Art Deco, including the magnificent 1938 Eden Theatre, now a hotel. Its facade contains a number of reliefs depicting scenes related to film, drama, and dance.

Opposite:
Detail,
decorative mural,
map of the North Atlantic.
Dining Room,
RMS Queen Mary,
1934.
1126 Queens Highway,
Long Beach, CA, USA.
Artist: MacDonald Gill.

Constructivist
granite wall plaque of
Vladimir Lenin.
Tverskaya Street,
Moscow, Russia.

The Soviet Union's
Constructivism of the
1920s and early '30s
grew out of
Russian Futurism.

This page and opposite:
Palais de Chaillot,
built for the 1937
Universal Exhibition.
1 Place du Trocadéro
et du 11 Novembre,
Paris, France.
Architects:
Louis-Hippolyte Boileau,
Jacques Carlu
and Léo Azéma.

Right:
Bull and Deer
bronze sculpture, 1937.
Jardin de Trocadéro,
Place du Trocadéro
et du 11 Novembre,
Paris, France.
Sculptor: Paul Jouve.

FRANCE

Horses and Dog
bronze sculpture, 1937.
Jardin de Trocadéro,
Place du Trocadéro
et du 11 Novembre,
Paris, France.
Sculptor: Georges Guyot.

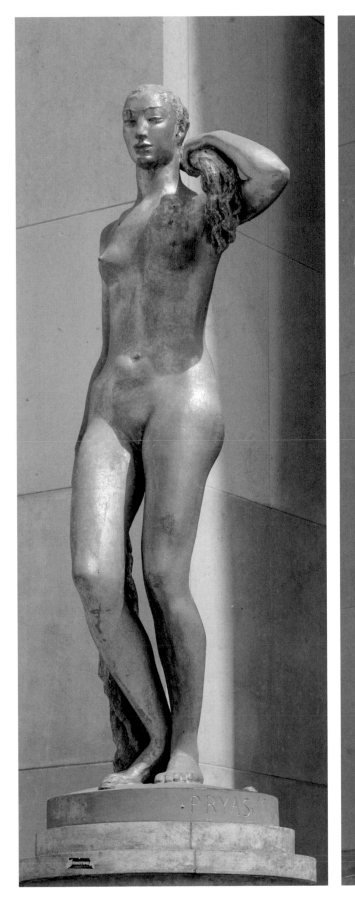

Above:
Stone boss, 1937.
Palais de Chaillot,
1 Place du Trocadéro
et du 11 Novembre,
Paris, France

Far left:
"Le matin".
Sculptor:
Jean Paris dit Pryas.
and left:
"La Jeunesse".
Sculptor:
Alexandre Descatoire.
Two gilded bronze
fountain sculptures, 1937.
Palais de Chaillot,
1 Place du Trocadéro
et du 11 Novembre,
Paris, France.

Right:
1930s "Flappers".
Keystone bas-reliefs,
private residence.
Paris, France.

Below:
Keystone bas-relief,
private residence.
Paris, France.
Sculptor:
Paul-Jacques-Aimé Baudry.

Above:
Detail, mosaic, facade,
Louxor Palais du Cinema,
1921,
170 Boulevard de Magenta,
Paris, France.
Architect:
Henri Zipcy.

Concrete facade,
Ornano 43 Theatre, 1930s.
43 Boulevard Ornano,
Paris, France.
Architect:
Marcel Oudin.

This page and opposite:
Details, facade,
Folies-Bergère, 1926.
Now restored in
gold leaf.
32 Rue Richer,
Paris, France.
Architect: Plumeret.
Artist: Maurice Picaud.

Detail, decorated frosted
glass door, main entrance,
Folies-Bergere, 1928.
32 Rue Richer,
Paris, France.

Right:
Bronze and
frosted glass door, 1930s.
Passage Jouffroy,
10 Boulevard Montmartre,
Paris, France.

Opposite:
Painted frosted
glass window, 1930s.
Passage Jouffroy,
10 Boulevard Montmartre,
Paris, France.

Above:
Detail, plaster wall decoration, café, 1930s. Paris, France.

Above and right:
Decorative metal
and glass doors, 1930s.
7th Arrondissement,
Paris, France.

Service entrance,
metal and
wired glass door,
private residence, 1930s.
Paris, France.

"Medecine" (Pharmacy)
metal store sign.
Now a Starbucks.
91 Boulevard Saint-Germain,
Paris, France.

Above and left:
Hanging metal sign,
facade,
metal window grilles,
Grande Pharmacie
du Centre, 1930s.
29 Place de la Cathédrale,
Rouen, France.
Ironwork:
Raymond Subes.

Right: Mosaic sign, horsemeat butcher shop, 1930s.
Now a clothing store.
Rue du Roi de Sicile, Paris, France.

Top:
Marble and metal sign,
butcher shop, 1930s.
28 Rue des Rosiers,
Paris, France.

Below:
Marble facade,
butchershop, 1930s.
Paris, France.

Creamery, 1930s.
25 Rue Danielle Casanova,
Paris, France.

Left:
Art Deco facade,
and below:
Detail, mosaic panel,
Samaritaine
department store, 1933.
19 Rue de la Monnaie,
Paris, France.
Architect: Henri Sauvage.

Left:
Sculptural relief,
Office de Tourisme Nice,
Cote d'Azur, 1930s.
5 Promenade des Anglais,
Nice, France.
Sculptor: Gerard Choain.

One of three bas-reliefs.
Sculpture depicts Paris'
Notre-Dame cathedral
and the Gare de Lyon
railway station.
The city of Nice is
represented by the
sea and vines.
Two female figures hold
the coat-of-arms of their
respective cities and
support the PLM board
(Paris-Lyon-Marseille),
the famous SNCF train.

Above:
Entrance,
Palais de la Méditerranée,
1929, Nice, France.

Right:
Palais de la Méditerranée,
1929.
Now a hotel.
13 Promenade des Anglais,
Nice, France.
Architects: Charles and
Marcel Dalmas.

Built for American
millionaire Frank Jay Gould
as a hotel, casino, theatre,
restaurant, and cocktail bar.

MÉDITERRANÉE

Overleaf:
Detail,
right-hand tower,
Palais de la Méditerranée,
13 Promenade des Anglais,
Nice, France.

Above:
Painted relief,
door portal, residence,
1930s.
Nice, France.

Howard Carter's
discovery of
Tutankhamun's Tomb
in 1922 sparked
a renewed interest
in Egyptology.

Right:
Decorative fountain,
wrought iron and
glass door, store, 1930s.
Nice, France.

Opposite:
Entrance door to
Le Magenta building,
1933.
2 Place Magenta,
Nice, France.

Above:
Mosaic,
ocean liners, 1930s.
Pavement, Nice.

Right:
Wrought iron balcony,
Hotel Martinez,
1929.
73 La Croisette,
Cannes, France.
Architects:
Charles Palmero,
Pierre Veuvenot.

Right:
Decorative metal balcony,
residential building.
Cannes, France.

Opposite:
Detail, mosaic,
fishmonger shopfront.
Cannes, France.

Above:
Stone low relief,
Thiers Post Office, 1931.

Right:
Thiers Post Office, 1931.
21 Avenue Thiers,
Nice, France.
Architect:
Guillaume Tronchet.

Leaded glass windows
display machinery,
Thiers Post Office, 1931.
21 Avenue Thiers,
Nice, France.
Architect:
Guillaume Tronchet.

Above:
Detail, PTT metal logotype,
Postes, télégraphes
et téléphones,
Thiers Post Office, 1931.

Right:
Detail, sandstone reliefs,
Thiers Post Office, 1931.
21 Avenue Thiers,
Nice, France.
Architect:
Guillaume Tronchet.

Sandstone relief,
Thiers Post Office, 1931.
21 Avenue Thiers,
Nice, France.
Architect:
Guillaume Tronchet.

Tiled signage,
La Poste Thiers
(Post Office), 1931.
21 Avenue Thiers,
Nice, France.
Architect:
Guillaume Tronchet.

THE NETHERLANDS

Wood and glass door,
formerly headquarters
for Gemeentetram
(Municipal Tramway
Company), 1921–23.
Stadhouderskade 1,
Amsterdam,
the Netherlands.
Architect:
Pieter Lucas Marnette.
Artist: Jan Derwig.

Wrought iron
and glass lamp,
Headquarters,
Gemeentetram
(Municipal Tramway
Company), 1921–23.
Stadhouderskade I,
Amsterdam,
the Netherlands.
Architect:
Pieter Lucas Marnette.
Artist: Jan Derwig.

Above:
Leaded glass window,
Amsterdam School
of Architecture, 1920s.
Amsterdam,
the Netherlands

Right:
Leaded glass windows
and wood facade,
store front,
Patisserie Holtkamp, 1928.
Vijzelgracht 15,
Amsterdam,
the Netherlands.
Architect: Piet Kramer.

Opposite:
Entrance,
Gebouw Batavia, 1920.
Prins Hendrikkade 84–85,
Amsterdam,
the Netherlands.
Architect: JH Slot.

Built between 1918 and 1920
for NV Batavia Arak
Maatschappij, a trading
company for arak from
Jakarta (formerly Batavia)
in then Dutch-India.

This page and opposite:
Granite sculptures of mythical figures decorate some of the 200 bridges designed by Piet L. Kramer. Amsterdam, the Netherlands. Sculptor: Johan Polet.

Above:
Stylized granite dolphins,
right:
A lion,
and below:
a crocodile,
bridge over Singelgracht at Leidseplein, 1925. Amsterdam, the Netherlands. Sculptor: Johan Polet.

Opposite:
A granite stylized figure, Raadhuisstraat over Keizersgracht, Amsterdam, the Netherlands. Sculptor: Hildo Krop.

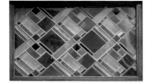

Above:
Leaded glass window, 1920s.
Amsterdam,
the Netherlands.

Right:
JJ van Noortschool,
1924–1925.
Prinsengracht 400,
Amsterdam,
the Netherlands.
Architect:
Cornelis Kruyswijk.
Artist: Theo van Reijn.

Above:
Street number,
Tuschinski Theatre, 1921.

Right:
Tuschinski Theatre, 1921.
Now Pathé Tuschinski.
Reguliersbreestraat 26–28,
Amsterdam,
the Netherlands.
Architect:
Heyman Louis de Jong.
Decorated by
Chris Bartels,
Jaap Gidding and
Pieter de Besten.

The theatre's founder,
Abraham Icek Tuschinski,
and most of his family,
were deported to a
concentration camp,
and eventually
died at Auschwitz.
For the duration of
the war, the theatre
was renamed "Tivoli".

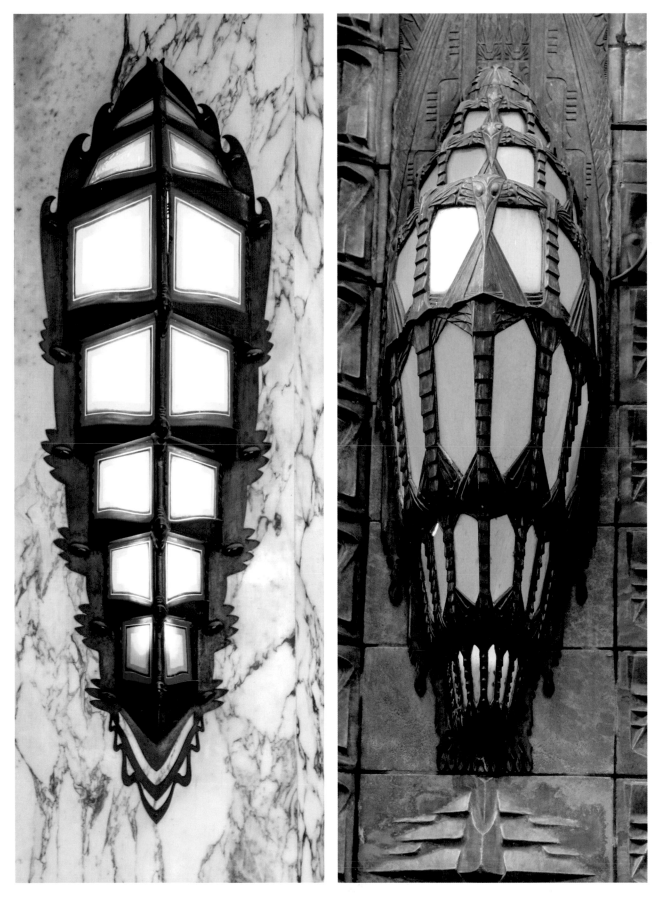

Two copper and colored
glass exterior light fixtures.
Tuschinski Theatre, 1921.
Reguliersbreestraat 26–28,
Amsterdam,
the Netherlands.

Above:
Glazed marble tiles,
Tuschinski Theatre, 1921.

Right:
Detail,
Tuschinski Theatre, 1921.
Reguliersbreestraat 26–28,
Amsterdam,
the Netherlands.
Architect:
Heyman Louis de Jong.
Decorated by
Chris Bartels,
Jaap Gidding and
Pieter de Besten.

Copper and glass
exterior sign,
Gerzon department
store, 1927.
Venestraat 36–38,
The Hague,
the Netherlands.
Architect:
Lodewijk Simons.

Leaded glass window,
Passage Theatre, 1930.
The Hague,
the Netherlands.

The Passage Theatre,
one of the oldest cinemas
in The Hague,
closed in 1986.

Above:
Bronze wall plaque,
De Bijenkorf
(The Beehive), 1926.

Right:
Leaded glass window,
De Bijenkorf
(The Beehive), 1926.
Grote Marktstraat 40,
The Hague,
the Netherlands.
Architect:
Piet Kramer.
Leaded glass:
M. Visser-Duker.

This page and opposite:
Examples of Art Deco
leaded glass windows,
1930s.
Brussels, Belgium.

BELGIUM

This page and opposite:
Four of twelve
stone medallions.
Images include the
Brooklyn Bridge, New York,
and a flying boat.
Stazione Marittima
(Port Terminal),
1934–1936.
Naples, Italy.
Architect: Cesare Bazzani.

Twin winged
Stazione Marittima
(Port Terminal),
1934–1936.
Naples, Italy.
Architect: Cesare Bazzani.

ITALY

Above:
One of four bronze
reliefs, depicting
the twin Greek
mythological brothers
Castor and Pollux.
Stazione Marittima
(Port Terminal), 1934–1936.

Note the shell-pocked
travestine marble facade
from the battle
for the liberation
of Naples, 1943.

Equestrian statue of
a mythical hippocampus.
Praça Imperio,
in the gardens of
Mosteiro dos Jerónimos,
Lisbon, Portugal.

PORTUGAL

Above:
Detail, marble paving,
map of Portugal,
Monument to the
Discoveries.
Belem, Lisbon, Portugal.

Left:
Padrão dos
Descobrimentos,
(Monument to the
Discoveries), 1939.
Belem, Lisbon, Portugal.
Architect: José Ângelo
Cottinelli Telmo.
Sculptor: Leopoldo
de Almeida.

The monument,
representing Portuguese
exploration, was originally
built as a temporary
structure for the 1940
Portuguese World Fair,
held in the
Praça do Império., Lisbon.
After the exhibition ended
in 1943, the monument
was destroyed.
It was eventually rebuilt
in its present location
overlooking the harbour.
Constructed in cement
and rose-tinted stone
(from Leiria), and the
statues sculpted from
limestone excavated
from the region of Sintra.
The new monument was
inaugurated in 1960.
Architect:
António Pardal Monteiro.
Sculptures modeled by
Leopoldo de Almeida.

Above:
Facade,
Teatro Cinearte, 1938.
Largo de Samos 2,
Lisbon, Portugal.
Architect:
Raul Rodriguez.
Now A Barraca Theatre.

After the building's closure
as a cinema it was
repurposed for a period
as a banana warehouse.

Right:
Eden Teatro, 1931.
Now a hotel.
Praça dos Restauradores 24,
Lisbon, Portugal.
Architects:
Cassiano Branco and
Carlo Florencio Dias.

The cinema closed in
1989 and lay unused for
many years. It was used
as a location in the
Wim Wenders movie
"Until the End of the World"
(1991).

Above:
Stone relief capital,
mask of Tragedy.
Eden Teatro, 1931.

Right:
Stone friezes depict
stylized actors performing
before a film crew,
Eden Teatro, 1931.
Now a hotel.
Praça dos Restauradores 24,
Lisbon, Portugal.
Architects:
Cassiano Branco and
Carlo Florencio Dias.

Cruise ship terminal,
Gare Marítima
de Alcântara, 1943.
Lisbon, Portugal.
Architect:
Pardal Monteiro.

The building's interior is
decorated with
large murals depicting
scenes of Portuguese
history, traditions,
and everyday life.
Artist:
José de Almada Negreiros.

PORTUGAL/SPAIN

Real Club Nautico de Vigo,
1945.
Rua Avenidas,
Vigo, Spain.
Architects:
Francisco Castro Represas
and Pedro Alonso Pérez.

Detail,
gilded pharmacy sign,
sandstone facade, 1910.
Frederiksberggade IA,
Copenhagen, Denmark.

DENMARK

Grundtvig's Church, 1921–1940.
På Bjerget 14B,
Bispebjerg,
Copenhagen, Denmark.
Architect:
Peder Vilhelm Jensen-Klint.

The design is a rare example
of expressionist church
architecture. Due to its
unusual appearance, it is
one of the best known
churches in the city.

Black vitrolite and
glass facade,
Daily Express newspaper
and printing plant, 1930–32.
Now Goldman Sachs
International.
120 Fleet Street,
London, UK.
Architects:
Sir Owen Williams
with Ellis and Clarke.

UNITED KINGDOM

Lobby,
silver and gilt lantern
and "Empire", one of two
plaster relief murals on
opposite sides of the
newspaper's entrance hall.
Designed by
Robert Atkinson.
Sculptor: Eric Aumonier.
Daily Express newspaper
and printing plant, 1930–32.
Now Goldman Sachs
International.
120 Fleet Street,
London, UK.

Below:
Main Lobby floor,
representing the ocean
separating Great Britain and
its Empire.
Daily Express building.

Overleaf:
"Britain", one of two
plaster relief murals.
Daily Express newspaper
and printing plant, 1930–32.
Sculptor: Eric Aumonier.

65

Above:
"Woman with cigarette",
Portland Stone facade,
one of four low reliefs,
Barkers department store,
1937–38.

Right:
One of two bronze
and glass towers.
Barkers department store,
1937–38.
Now a
fashion store complex.
63 Kensington High Street,
London, UK.
Architect: Bernard George.

Opposite:
Detail, glass block tower.
Barkers department store,
1937–38.
63 Kensington High Street
London, UK.
Architect: Bernard George.

Images in this low relief
montage include a
futuristic Delta-wing
jet engine aircraft.
Other panels include
an airship,
Oliver Bulleid's 1937
LMS Pacific Locomotive,
plus an array of
household goods.

Detail, cast bronze
relief spandrels
depicting store products,
Barkers department store,
1937–38.
Now a
fashion store complex.
63 Kensington High Street,
London, UK.
Architect: Bernard George.
Right:
Chair.
Below:
Cricket pads and stumps.

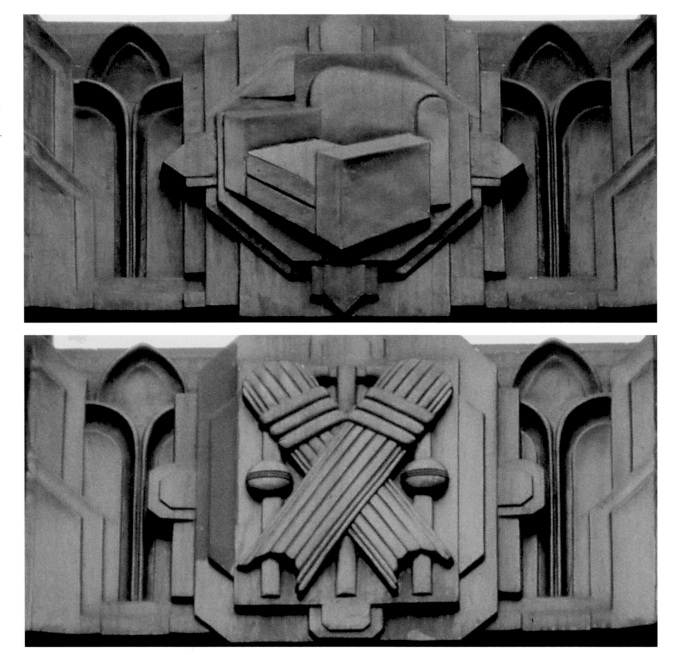

Right:
Cast aluminium frieze panel.
Derry & Toms
department store, 1933.
Now Marks & Spencer
department store.
99 Kensington High Street,
London, UK.
Architect: Bernard George.
Sculptor: Walter Gilbert.
Produced by:
The Bromsgrove Guild.

A one and a half acre
roof garden,
added in 1936–38,
hosts live flamingos.

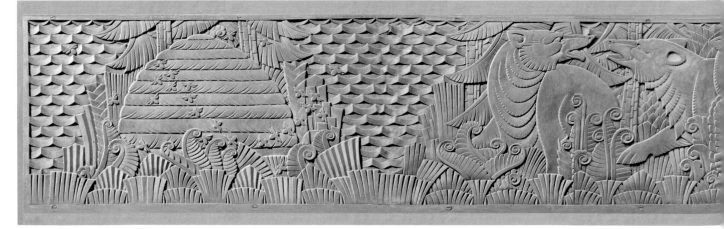

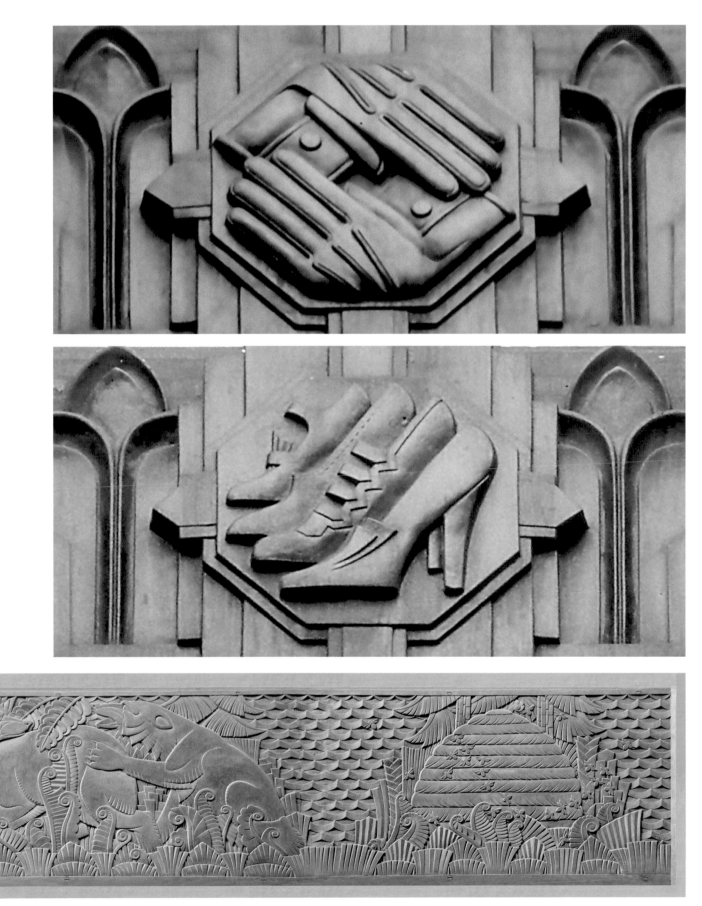

Detail, cast bronze
relief spandrels
depicting store products,
Barkers department store,
1937–38.
Now a
fashion store complex.
63 Kensington High Street,
London, UK.
Architect: Bernard George.
Left:
Gloves,
Below:
Shoes.

Opposite:
"Father Thames",
Great West Road
entrance,
Hammersmith Town Hall,
1939.
I Riverside Gardens,
Hammersmith,
London, UK.
Architect:
E. Berry Webber.
Sculptor:
George Alexander.

Above and left:
Mosaics, canopy.
Poplar Borough Council
coat-of-arms plus figures
representing the arts.
Bow Town Hall, 1937–38.

Two of five Portland Stone
bas-relief panels.
Bow Town Hall, 1937–38.
Sculptor:
David Evans.

Sculptures depict the
workers who created the
building, including a welder,
a labourer, a mason, a
carpenter and an architect.

Above:
Detail, tiled cornice,
Hoover Factory,
1931–35.

Right:
West wing tower,
Hoover Factory,
1931–35.
Now a supermarket.
Western Avenue,
Perivale, Middx, UK.
Architects:
Wallis, Gilbert
and Partners.

The location was chosen
for its access to the
Great Western Railway
and docks for distribution
of the Hoover
vacuum cleaners.
The building's exterior was
constructed using
"Snowcrete"
(a white concrete
which stays white in spite
of the British weather).
It is decorated with bright
colored faience ceramic
Egyptian-inspired tiles.

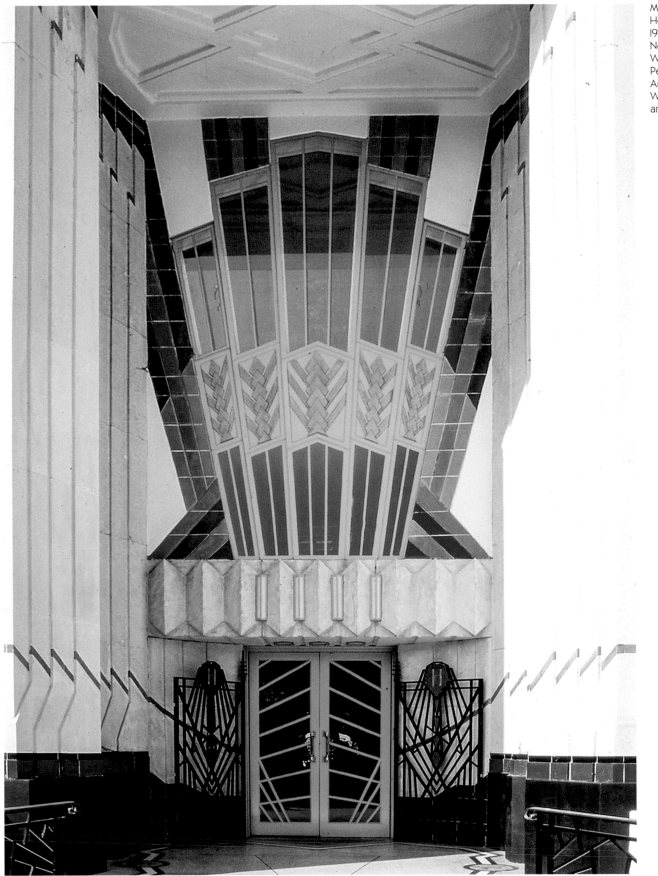

Main entrance,
Hoover Factory,
1931–35.
Now a supermarket.
Western Avenue,
Perivale, Middx, UK.
Architects:
Wallis, Gilbert
and Partners.

Above:
Ship finial,
washing line post,
Doulton stoneware,
1926.
St. Nicholas' Flats,
Sidney Street Estate,
Somerstown, London N1.
Sculptor:
Gilbert Bayes.

Top right:
The Princess
and the Swineherd,
Grimms Fairy Tales.
Doulton glazed
ceramic Lunettes, 1926.
Sidney Street Estate,
Somerstown, London N1.
Sculptor:
Gilbert Bayes.

Right;
The Sleeping Beauty
with Prince,
Hans Christian Anderson.
Doulton glazed
ceramic Lunettes, 1926.
Sidney Street Estate,
Somerstown, London N1.
Sculptor:
Gilbert Bayes

Drama, Adventure,
Romance, Terpsichore.
Doulton Polychrome
stoneware.
White Rock Pavilion,
Hastings, 1927.
Sculptor:
Gilbert Bayes.

Overleaf:
"Pottery Through the Ages"
Detail, 50-ft polychrome
stoneware frieze,
facade of the former
Royal Doulton's
Doulton House, 1939.
Lambeth, London, UK.
Now in the collection of the
Victoria & Albert Museum,
London.
Sculptor: Gilbert Bayes.
With kind permission of
the Gilbert Bayes
Charitable Trust.

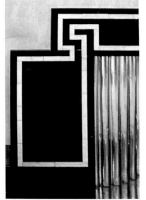

Above:
Detail, Greek meander-
inspired fireplace
decoration, dining room,
Eltham Palace, 1936.

Right:
Entrance Hall,
Eltham Palace, 1936.
Eltham, Greenwich, UK.
Architects:
Seely and Paget.
Designer: Rolf Engströmer.

A medieval and
Tudor Palace,
the former home
of King Henry VIII,
was converted
in the 1930s in
the Art Deco style
into the private home of
Stephen and Virginia
Courtauld.

Opposite:
Gold mosaic tiles
and marble bath,
Virgina Courtald's
bathroom.
Eltham Palace, 1936.

AUSTRALASIA

Above:
Detail, "Platypus"
leaded glass skylight,
National Museum of
Australian Zoology, 1930.
Now National Film and
Sound Archive of Australia.
McCoy Circuit,
Canberra, Australia.
Architect:
Walter Hayward Morris.

Opposite:
Detail of the three-part
glass mosaic entitled
"I'll Put A Girdle Round
About The Earth".
Former Newspaper House,
1933.
247-249 Collins Street,
Melbourne, Australia.
Architects:
Stephenson & Meldrum.
Artist:
Mervyn Napier Waller.

Mosaic floor, lobby,
State Theatre, 1929.
49 Market St,
Sydney, NSW, Australia.
Architect:
Henry Eli White.

My first visit "Down Under" was in 1998, at the invitation of the Australian Graphic Designers Association, to undertake a lecture tour of their far-flung chapters in Perth, Western Australia, and on to Melbourne, Canberra, Sydney, and Brisbane in New South Wales and Queensland.

I found a variance in the styles of each city's architecture. In Perth, sandstone kookaburra ornaments abound adorning their suburban gardens and reflecting the laid-back demeanor of its citizens. Melbourne still embraces its Imperial architectural past with bold flourishes of Art Deco, notably the mosaic facade of the former Newspaper House created by Melvyn Napier Waller.

I discovered Sydney to be a bouquet of Deco delights. Among the city's colorful examples is Lunar Park, the amusement park located at Milsons Point on the northern shore of the Sydney Harbour Bridge.

Another highlight of the city's 1930s architecture is the magnificent ANZAC Memorial. Designed by architect C. Bruce Dellit, its exterior is adorned with monumental figurative reliefs, sculpted by Rayner Hoff, plus his two ten-meter-long bronze panoramas depicting the Imperial Forces activities on the Western and Eastern fronts during the First World War.

Another of my favorite Art Deco buildings is the Metropolitan Water Sewerage and Drainage Board Building, with its bronze facade sculpted by Stanley James Hammond. The building is now a luxury hotel.

On my visit to the National Film and Sound Archive of Australia in Canberra, I was pleasantly surprised to note in the reception's leaded glass skylight a depiction of a Platypus, one of the continent's indigenous mammals.

With the knowledge that my wife and I were scheduled to visit Auckland, New Zealand, for just one day during one of my cruise ship lecture tours, I contacted the president of Auckland's Art Deco Society who graciously agreed to acquaint us with the city and its suburbs' finest examples of Art Deco.

Meeting us at the dock she gave us the grand tour, from the many beautiful Moderne white residential homes to several cinemas, to a sculpted couple of bronze monsters decorating a fountain, plus a visit to New Zealand's vast ANZAC Memorial, decorated with sculptural figures and reliefs of military service personnel, as is the World War One memorial in Sydney.

We completed our tour with a visit to Auckland's Civic Theatre in the heart of the city prior to returning to our ship.

On my wish-list for a future trip to New Zealand is a visit to the city of Napier, which was rebuilt in the Art Deco style after the devastating Hawke's Bay earthquake in 1931.

Above:
Entrance,
Luna Park, 1935.
Sydney, NSW, Australia.

AUSTRALIA

Right:
One of two towers of
the amusement park.
Olympic Drive,
Milsons Point,
Sydney, NSW, Australia.

The tower's design
was inspired by
New York's Chrysler Building.

Tiled signage,
former Broadway Hotel,
Chippendale,
Sydney, NSW, Australia.

Stone relief
decorative frogs.
North Sydney
Olympic Pool,
Milsons Point,
Sydney, NSW, Australia.

Former Buckley's
Buckley & Nunn Ltd
Men's store, 1933.
294–296 Bourke Street,
Melbourne, Australia.
Architects:
Bates, Smart
and McCutcheon.

Above:
Detail,
sculptural figure
The ANZAC Memorial,
1934.

Right:
Memorial and
reflecting pool,
The ANZAC Memorial,
1934.
Hyde Park,
Sydney, NSW, Australia.
Architect:
C. Bruce Dellit.
Sculptor: Rayner Hoff.

This is the main ANZAC
(Australian and
New Zealand Army Corps)
commemorative
monument,
Sydney, Australia.

Opposite:
Facade,
The ANZAC Memorial,
1934.
Hyde Park,
Sydney, NSW, Australia.
Architect:
C. Bruce Dellit.
Sculptor: Rayner Hoff.

Above:
"Apollo,"
J.F. Archibald
Memorial Fountain,
bronze, 1932.
Hyde Park,
Sydney, NSW, Australia.
Sculptor:
François-Léon Sicard.

Top right:
"The Eastern Campaigns".
One of two
bronze panels,
Anzac War Memorial, 1934.
Hyde Park,
Sydney, NSW, Australia.
Sculptor: Rayner Hoff.

Each panel is
ten meters wide
by one meter high.

Below right:
"The noblest of the
elements is water."
— Pindar
Metropolitan Water
Sewerage & Drainage
Board building, 1939.
Now a hotel.
339 Pitt Street,
Sydney, NSW, Australia.
Architects:
H.E. Budden and Mackey.
Sculptor:
Stanley James Hammond.

Above:
Metro Theatre.
Originally Minerva Theatre,
1939.
28 Orwell Street.
Potts Point, Sydney,
NSW, Australia.
Architect: Bruce Dellit.

This page and opposite:
Hayden Orpheum
Picture Palace, 1935.
380 Military Rd,
Cremorne, Sydney,
NSW, Australia.
Architect:
George Kenworthy.

Top:
Ceiling light fixture.
Hayden Orpheum
Picture Palace, 1935.

Right:
Terazzo floors.
Hayden Orpheum
Picture Palace, 1935.

Opposite:
Theatre lobby.
Hayden Orpheum
Picture Palace, 1935.

The Maritime Services
Board building.
Now the Museum of
Contemporary Art.
Designed in 1939–1940,
and built 1949–1952.
140 George Street,
Sydney, NSW, Australia.
Architect:
William Henry Withers.

The building's exterior
is constructed of
sandstone cladding.

Opposite:
"I'll Put A Girdle Round
 About The Earth".
Detail of glass mosaic.
Former Newspaper House,
1933.
247–249 Collins Street,
Melbourne, Australia.
Architect:
Stephenson & Meldrum.

Right:
Granite bas-relief
above the building's
main entrance.
The Maritime Services
Board building.
Designed in 1939–1940,
and built 1949–1952.
Now the Museum of
Contemporary Art.
Sydney, NSW, Australia.
Sculptor:
Lyndon Raymond Dadswell.

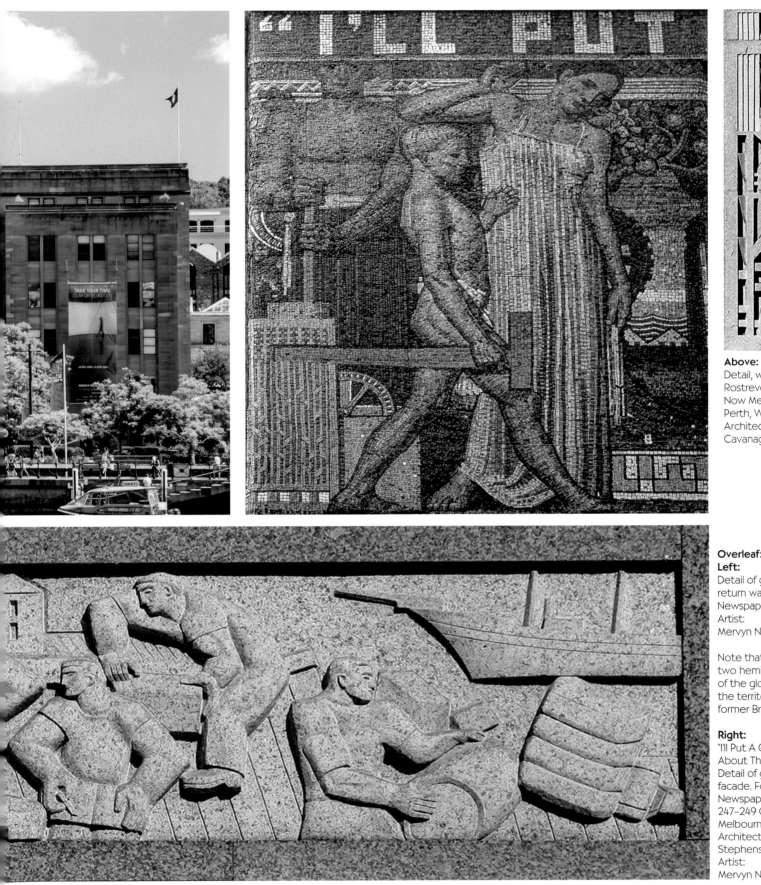

Above:
Detail, wall decoration,
Rostrevor Flats, 1937.
Now Mercedes College.
Perth, Western Australia.
Architects:
Cavanagh and Cavanagh.

Overleaf:
Left:
Detail of glass mosaic,
return wall. Former
Newspaper House, 1933.
Artist:
Mervyn Napier Waller.

Note that the
two hemispheres
of the globes show in red
the territories of the
former British Empire.

Right:
"I'll Put A Girdle Round
About The Earth".
Detail of glass mosaic
facade. Former
Newspaper House, 1933.
247–249 Collins Street,
Melbourne, Australia.
Architects:
Stephenson & Meldrum.
Artist:
Mervyn Napier Waller.

Trevor Moss Davis
Memorial fountain, 1950 .
Mission Bay Reserve,
Auckland, New Zealand.
Architect: George Tole.
Created by
Lancashire-born
Richard Gross.

NEW ZEALAND

Auckland
Central Fire Station, 1944.
40 Pitt Street,
Auckland, New Zealand.
Architect:
Daniel B. Patterson.

The Civic Theatre, 1929.
Queen Street and
Wellesley Street,
Auckland, New Zealand.
Architects:
Charles Bohringer
and William T. Leighton.

The Civic Theatre narrowly
escaped demolition in
1988 thanks to a
High Court injunction.
It was restored
by the Auckland City
Council and reopened on
December 20, 1999,
the 70th anniversary
of its first performance.

THE AMERICAS

My romance with all things American began with my father's copies of the Saturday Evening Post. These magazines came with the compliments of the American servicemen who frequented the Savoy Hotel. The magazine's realistic cover illustrations by Norman Rockwell introduced me to the world of Streamline design, including automobiles, radios, and home appliances. The pages were in stark contrast to the advertisements in the British wartime magazines such as Picture Post and Lilliput, which were mostly related to utility clothing and the Home Front.

An invitation to receive an award at the Dominican Republic's "Festival de Cine Global Dominicano" afforded me the opportunity to stop over in Miami in order to photograph some of the world's most revered examples of Art Deco and Moderne architecture.

Despite the devastating havoc wrought upon the Americas by hurricanes and earthquakes, thankfully South Beach's structures are still intact.

On-location filming in San Juan, Puerto Rico, plus invitations from film festivals in South America's Montevideo, Uruguay, Panama City, Panama, and Mexico's Guadalajara have presented me with the opportunity to photograph further examples of the Art Deco and Moderne style.

Attendance at a film premiere in Boston gave me another opportunity to photograph great examples of Art Deco architecture and its details, such as the magnificent gilded panels of the 75 Federal Street building, and the facade of the Shoe Manufacturers Building.

My first visit to the United States was to New York in 1978. From the observation deck of the Empire State Building, I was able to survey the vast sprawling skyline of Manhattan, which so much resembled the poster that hangs on our dining room wall for Fritz Lang's 1927 Machine Age masterpiece film, "Metropolis".

I felt that I already knew the town and the Empire State Building from the films that I had seen, such as "King Kong" and "On The Town". Through the haze I was able to spot the gleaming silver spire of the 1928 Chrysler Building. My photograph of the spectacular Art Deco Airlines Terminal Building was taken just prior to its demolition in 1978.

My favorite location is Rockefeller Center, which is adorned with a multitude of sculptural delights by Lee Lawrie, whose work I later photographed for one of my books.

My departure from Manhattan for the airport was via helicopter from the rooftop of the Pan Am Building; from mid-air I was able to photograph the Empire State Building.

Fortunately it was not to be my last visit to New York, so I have had the opportunity to continue my architectural exploration of the city over the following years.

In 1978 I was invited to work in Los Angeles, the town where the "Dream Factories" produced all those glamorous 1930s Busby Berkeley Art Deco fantasies, which I assume drew some of their inspiration from the city's fine examples of Art Deco architecture.

Los Angeles' most prominent architect of the day was Lancashire-born John Parkinson. He was responsible for many of the city's most iconic buildings, including City Hall, Union Station, the Los Angeles Memorial Coliseum, plus the "Jewel in the Crown", Bullocks Wilshire department store, which Parkinson designed along with his son Donald.

We are blessed in Los Angeles to have no fewer than three structures designed by one of the great universally recognized pioneers of modern architecture, Frank Lloyd-Wright.

Los Angeles has been my home for the past forty years, and continues to provide me with the pleasures of discovering further Art Deco gems which I celebrated in my books "Deco Landmarks: Art Deco Gems of Los Angeles"; "Griffith Observatory, A Celebration of its Architectural Splendor"; and "Los Angeles Central Library, A History of its Art and Architecture", co-authored with Stephen Gee.

Opposite:
Detail,
decorative mural,
map of the North Atlantic.
Dining Room,
RMS Queen Mary, 1934.
1126 Queens Highway,
Long Beach, CA, USA.
Artist: MacDonald Gill.

Above:
Leaded glass window,
"Centro Comercial
Colón", 1930s.
Calle El Conde,
Santo Domingo,
Dominican Republic.

Above:
Detail, copper zodiac sign,
"Aquarius,
the Water Carrier",
door panel,
Finnish Consulate.

URUGUAY

Right and top:
Two stone
sculpted figures.
Finnish Consulate, 1930s.
Now J.R. Willams
port agents.
Calle Solis 1533,
Montevideo, Uruguay.
Architects:
J. Herran and L. Crespi.

One of two bronze doors
inset with copper
Zodiac signs,
Finnish Consulate, 1930s.

Above, top and opposite:
Apartment building entrance, 1931.
1390 Juan Carlos Gomez,
Plaza Matriz,
Montevideo, Uruguay.
Architects:
G. Vázquez Barrière
and R. Ruano.

Centre:
Leaded glass window,
840 18 de Julio Avenida,
Montevideo, Uruguay.

Below:
Decorative metal grille
over doorway.
840 18 de Julio Avenida,
Montevideo, Uruguay.

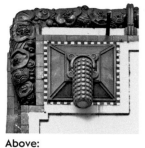

Above:
Tiled corner decoration,
and right:
Floral tile decoration,
facade,
Inter-American
Association of
Broadcasters.
Calle Carlos Quijano 1264,
Montevideo, Uruguay.

Right:
Metal door,
apartment building,
1930s.
Circunvalación Durango
1409,
Montevideo, Uruguay.

Far right:
Entrance,
apartment building,
1930s,
Calle San José 924,
Montevideo, Uruguay.

Opposite:
Three bas-relief figures
representing
Work, Saving, Commerce.
Banco La Caja Obrera,
1941.
Now an
apartment building.
25 de Mayo 500,
Montevideo, Uruguay.
Sculptor: Edmundo Prati.

SAN JOSE PALACE

TRABAJO   AHORRO   COMERCIO

Brass lottery balls
surround a
lottery ball cage.
Main entrance,
Lotería Nacional
Building, 1936.
(National Lottery)
Plaza de la Reforma
Mexico City, Mexico.
Architect:
José Antonio Cuevas.

The 18-story structure
was the first building
to use elastic floatation
for earthquake protection.

MEXICO

"M. Lambert",
leaded glass window,
Mexico City, Mexico.

Brass on marble signs.
Top:
"Taquilla" (Ticket Office),
Below:
"Descuentos" (Discounts),
Palacio de Bellas Artes,
1934.
(Palace of Fine Arts).
Avenida Juárez,
Mexico City, Mexico,
Architect:
Federico Mariscal.

Construction commenced
in 1904 in the
Art Nouveau style.
However, due to the
Mexican Revolution
of 1910, work was
suspended.
Building resumed in
1931 under the direction
of architect Federico
Mariscal, which accounts
for the museum's
Art Deco interior.

Above:
Facade,
mosaic signage,
Puerto de Veracruz
department store,
Mexico City, Mexico.

Above:
"CQD",
carved wooden plaque
featuring crickets,
Casa Quiñones, 1930.

This page and opposite:
Casa Quiñones, 1930.
Avenida La Paz 2219,
Guadalajara, Mexico.
Architect:
Pedro
Castellanos Lambley.

Opposite:
Metal and glass door,
Casa Quiñones, 1930.

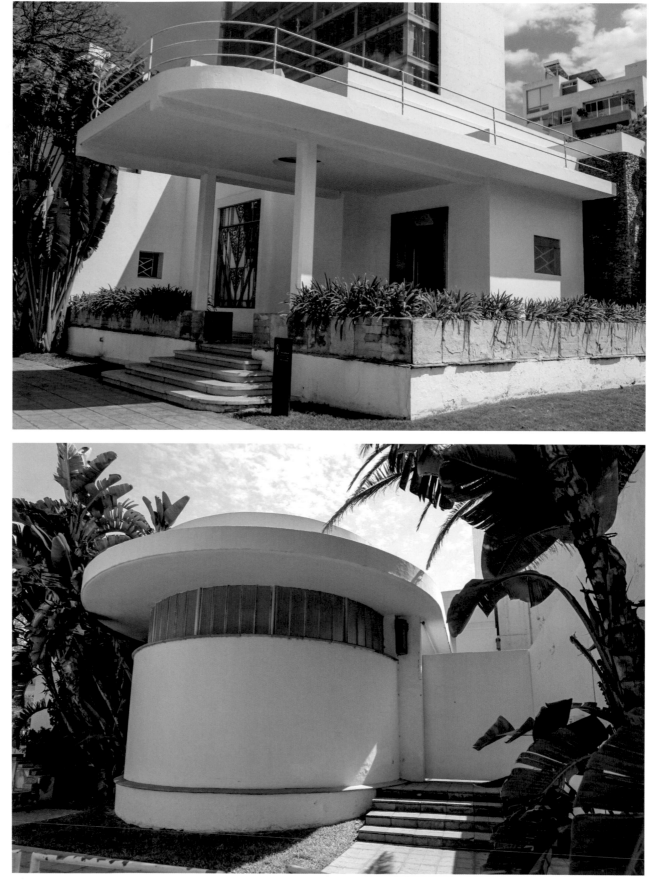

Sculptures of
ancient Gods,
facade,
Banco Popular de
Puerto Rico, 1938.
206 Calle de Tetuán,
San Juan, Puerto Rico.
Architect:
Osvaldo Toro.

PUERTO RICO

SERVICIO
O·RICO 1938

DE PUERTO RICO

Above:
Detail, tiled facade,
Polo Norte
Fabrica de Sodas.
Calle de Tetuán,
San Juan, Puerto Rico.

Terracotta and
copper tower,
Bullocks Wilshire
department store, 1929.
Now the Southwestern
Law School.
3050 Wilshire Boulevard,
Los Angeles, CA, USA.
Architects:
John and Donald Parkinson.

UNITED STATES

Above:
One of several wall clocks,
Bullocks Wilshire
department store, 1929.

Left:
"The Spirit of
Transportation".
Detail, ceiling fresco, winged
messenger
"Mercury".
Porte cochère,
Bullocks Wilshire
department store, 1929.
Westmoreland Street
entrance.
Muralist: Hermann Sachs.

Detail, woven carpet.
Bullocks Wilshire
department store, 1929.

Above:
Metal signage,
Bullock's Wilshire
later Bullocks Wilshire
department store, 1929.

Right:
Facade,
terracotta relief,
Bullocks Wilshire
department store, 1929.
Now the Southwestern Law
School.
Wilshire Boulevard
entrance.
3050 Wilshire Boulevard,
Los Angeles, CA, USA.
Architects:
John and Donald Parkinson.
Sculptor: George Stanley.

Note the similarity
between the figures
on the left and Stanley's
design of the Oscar®
statuette.

TO BVILD A B
NEVER KN

Above:
Copper clock, lobby.
Bullocks Wilshire
department store, 1929.

This page and opposite:
Interior,
Bullocks Wilshire
department store, 1929.
Now the Southwestern
Law School.
3050 Wilshire Boulevard,
Los Angeles, CA, USA.
Architects:
John and Donald Parkinson.

Right:
Glazed tiles
drinking fountain.

Opposite:
Elevator door.
Metal inlays of brass,
copper and gunmetal,
plus various
wood veneers.
Designer: Jock D. Peters.

"A cathedral to commerce".
Donald Parkinson attended
the Paris Exposition in 1925
and was so taken by the
new style of architecture
that he abandoned the
original plans for the
department store. He and
his father, John Parkinson,
eventually produced one
of the world's most
outstanding examples
of the Art Deco style.

Above:
Detail, bronze figure points down to the globe, The Globe Lobby, Los Angeles Times Building, 1935.

Right:
Native American, one of several bronze reliefs, surrounding the globe's base, Los Angeles Times Mirror Building, 1935, a PWA (Public Works Administration) Moderne building. 202 W. First Street and Spring Street, Los Angeles, CA, USA. Architect: Gordon B. Kaufmann. Muralist: Hugo Balin.

The Globe Lobby,
Los Angeles Times
Mirror Building, 1935

The Los Angeles Times
circular lobby's
aluminum globe
emulates the 1930
giant globe in
The News Building,
New York City.

The globe completes a
rotation every five minutes.
Surrounding the base
are bronze bas-reliefs
symbolizing industry,
religion, science and art
along with minor reliefs
representing the American
Indian, the Greek scholar,
the Zulu warrior, and the
Chinese Mandarin.

Hugo Balin's 10-ft. high
murals depict scenes
from Los Angeles and
the newspaper industry.

Hugo Balin's murals
can be seen in many
prestigious buildings
throughout Los Angeles.
Balin also worked as an art
director, writer, director
and producer in over
one hundred silent films.

Above:
"Oil",
one of twelve bronze
panels above the
Los Angeles Times
Mirror Building's
main entrance depicting
the various topics
covered by the newspaper.

Right:
Details,
bronze signage,
Los Angeles Times
Mirror Building, 1935,
a PWA (Public Works
Administration)
Moderne building.
202 W. First Street
and Spring Street,
Los Angeles, CA USA.
Architect:
Gordon B. Kaufmann.

Mailbox,
lobby,
Los Angeles Times
Building, 1935.

Above:
Cast concrete relief,
facade,
Allan Hancock
Foundation Building,
1940.

This page and opposite:
Pleistocene mammals,
facade decoration,
Allan Hancock
Foundation Building,
1940.
University of Southern
California Campus,
Los Angeles, CA USA.
Architects:
C. Raimond Johnson
and Samuel Lunde.
Sculptor: Merrell Gage.

Facade and entrance,
Allan Hancock
Foundation Building,
1940.
University of Southern
California Campus,
Los Angeles, CA USA.
Architects:
C. Raimond Johnson
and Samuel Lunde.

The building's exterior,
built in the
Late Moderne style,
includes sculptures of a
variety of animals and
plant life seen along the
Pacific basin during the
exploratory cruises of
Captain Allan Hancock.

Above:
One of a number of
pavement terrazzo floor
medallions depicting
Los Angeles landmarks,
Cliftons Brookdale
Cafeteria, 1936.
648 S. Broadway,
Los Angeles, CA, USA.

Right:
Griffith Park Observatory,
1935.
View from the south,
looking north.
2800 East Observatory
Road, Griffith Park,
Los Angeles, CA, USA.
Architects: John C. Austin
and F.M. Ashley.

Front prospect, at night,
Griffith Park Observatory,
1935.

The Observatory was
featured in the 1955 film
"Rebel Without a Cause"
starring James Dean,
as well as the
2016 film "La La Land".

124

Top left:
Sunset,
archway overlooking
the Hollwood sign.
Griffith Park Observatory,
1935.

Top right:
Griffith Park Observatory
Astronomers Monument.
Griffith Park Observatory,
1935.

The 40-foot-high cast
concrete fluted obelisk
monument honours the
legendary pioneers in
astronomical achievements.
Funded through the New
Deal initiative's Public
Works of Art Project
(PWAP) and the
Women's Auxiliary of
the Los Angeles Chamber
of Commerce.
Designer: Archibald Garner.
Garner and five other
sculptors created
the figures.

George Stanley,
one of the
monument's sculptors,
also created the bas-relief
above the entrance of
Bullocks Wilshire, the
Hollywood Bowl entry
fountain, and the
Oscar® statuette.

Above:
Detail, one of a number
of bronze symbols
decorating the
Observatory's front
entrance gates.

Above:
Unglazed terracotta tiles decorate the fountain's pavement.

Right:
"Electric Fountain," 1931.
Corner of Wilshire and Santa Monica Boulevards,
Beverly Hills, CA, USA.
Designer:
Ralph C. Flewelling.
Sculptor:
Robert Merrell Gage.

Opposite:
"Muse of Music" sculpture, 1929.
Two of three granite figures representing music, drama and dance, a WPA project.
Hollywood Bowl,
2301 N. Highland Avenue,
Los Angeles, CA, USA.
Sculptor:
George Stanley.

Above:
White metal mallechort
letterbox.
Designer:
René Lalique.

This page and opposite:
Alexander & Oviatt
haberdashery store,
1927-28.
617 S. Olive Street,
Los Angeles, CA, USA.
Architects:
Walker and Eisen

Top left:
Oviatt Building
Lalique glass
elevator doors.

Top right:
Oviatt Building
entrance gate.

Below:
Metal and glass
entrance canopy.

On James Oviatt's visit to
the 1925 Paris Exposition
Internationale des
Arts Decoratifs et
Industriels Modernes,
he was impressed by
seeing René Lalique's
"The Springs of France"
glass fountain.
This inspired Oviatt to
commission Lalique
to design elements
for his new store.

Oviatt Building
entrance gate detail.

Above:
"Moses",
bas-relief keystone,
main entrance.
Hollywood–Western
Building, 1928.

Right:
Bas-relief,
"Winged Mercury"
holding a film camera,
underside of balcony,
Hollywood–Western
Building, 1928.
Western Avenue and
Hollywood Boulevard,
Los Angeles, CA, USA.
Architect:
S. Charles Lee.

Far right:
Bas-relief stone figures
above the entrance
depict directors,
producers and architects.
Hollywood–Western
Building, 1928.
Western Avenue and
Hollywood Boulevard,
Los Angeles, CA, USA.
Architect:
S. Charles Lee.

Below:
The building's
fire escapes
are decorated
with bas-relief
classic Greek figures
and a film crew.

These nude figures
ironically appeared
outside film censor
Will Hayes' office
("the Tsar of all
the Rushes").
The building was
constructed for MGM
mogul Louis B. Mayer,
and opened by
Norma Shearer
and Irving Thalberg.

Graumann's
Chinese Theatre, 1927.
Now
TCL Chinese Theatre.
6925 Hollywood
Boulevard,
Los Angeles, CA, USA.
Architects:
Meyer and Holler.

There are hundreds of
Hollywood celebrity
handprints, footprints,
and autographs in
the concrete of the
Chinese Theatre's
forecourt, known as the
"Forecourt of the stars".
The first to place
their handprints
were Norma Talmadge,
Mary Pickford, and
Douglas Fairbanks.

Fox Bruin Theatre, 1937.
Now
Regency Village Theatre.
926–950 Broxton
Boulevard,
Los Angeles, CA, USA.
Architect: S. Charles Lee.

Above:
Detail, terrazzo floor,
El Rey Theatre, 1936.
Now a live music venue.
5515 Wilshire Boulevard,
Los Angeles, CA, USA.
Architect: Clifford Balch.

Left:
Theater box office,
Alex Theatre, 1942.
216 N. Brand Boulevard,
Glendale, CA, USA.
Architect: S. Charles Lee.

Theater box office,
Culver Theatre, 1946.
Now
Kirk Douglas Theatre,
9820 Washington
Boulevard,
Culver City, CA, USA.

Overleaf left:
Alex Theatre, 1942.
216 N. Brand Boulevard,
Glendale, CA, USA.
Architect: S. Charles Lee.

Overleaf right:
"Streamline Moderne"
Academy Theatre, 1938.
Inglewood, CA, USA.
Architect: S. Charles Lee.

The Academy Theatre
was planned to be used
for the Academy
Awards. An etched-glass
figure of a woman holding
an Oscar adorns the light-
trap door. However, the
theatre was never used
for that purpose.

Orpheum Theatre, 1926.
842 S. Broadway,
Los Angeles, CA, USA.
Architects:
G. Albert Lansburgh,
Robert Brown Young.

Alex Theatre, 1942.
216 N. Brand Boulevard,
Glendale, CA, USA.
Architect: S. Charles Lee.

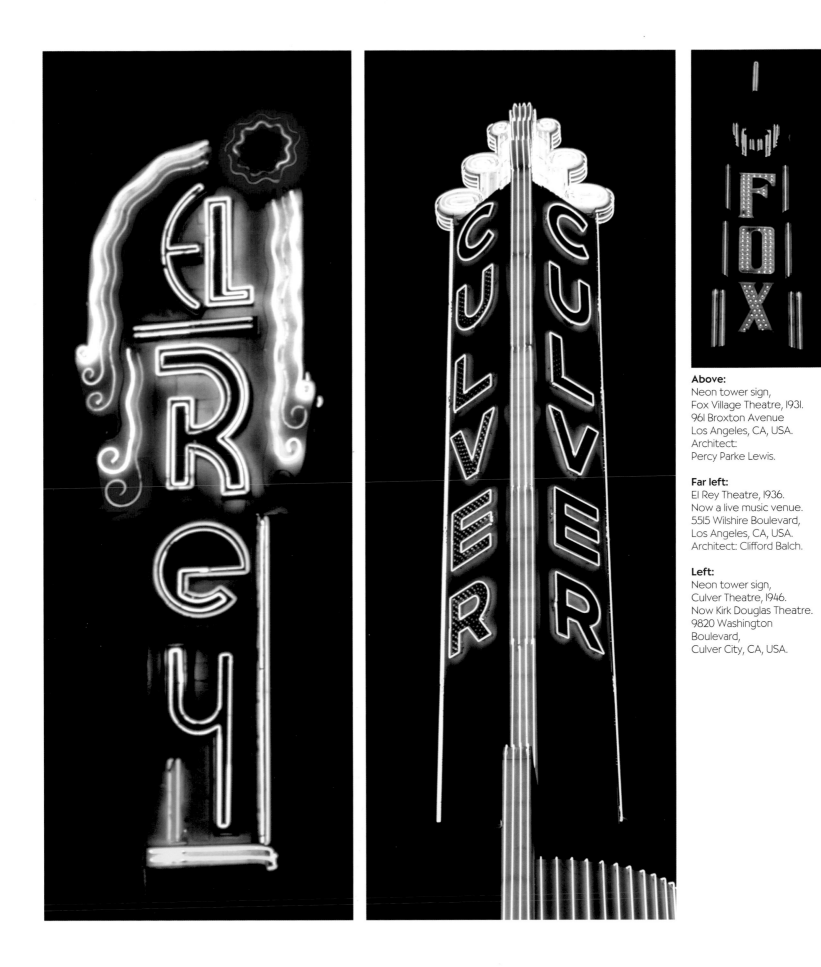

Above:
Neon tower sign,
Fox Village Theatre, 1931.
961 Broxton Avenue
Los Angeles, CA, USA.
Architect:
Percy Parke Lewis.

Far left:
El Rey Theatre, 1936.
Now a live music venue.
5515 Wilshire Boulevard,
Los Angeles, CA, USA.
Architect: Clifford Balch.

Left:
Neon tower sign,
Culver Theatre, 1946.
Now Kirk Douglas Theatre.
9820 Washington
Boulevard,
Culver City, CA, USA.

137

"Santa Fe All The Way".
Union Station, 1939.
800 N. Alameda Street,
Los Angeles, CA, USA.
Architects:
John and Donald Parkinson.

The railway station is a blend of Spanish Revival and Streamlined Moderne architectural styles.

Right:
Main waiting area,
Union Station, 1939.

Below:
Tiles produced by Gladding, McBean & Co.,
Fred Harvey Room,
Union Station, 1939.

Right:
Facade,
Union Station, 1939.

Opposite:
West facade,
Los Angeles
Central Library, 1926.
630 W. Fifth Street,
Los Angeles, CA, USA.
Architect:
Bertram Goodhue.
Sculptor: Lee Lawrie.

Lee Lawrie was responsible for much of the sculptural work at New York's Rockefeller Center.

Dean Cornwell's magnificent murals in the Library's rotunda were painted in Kensington, London.

Above:
Neon entry sign,
Crossroads of The World,
1936.

Right:
Revolving neon globe,
Crossroads of the World,
1936.
6671 Sunset Boulevard,
Los Angeles, CA, USA.
Architect:
Robert V. Derrah.

Designed in the
Streamline Moderne style
resembling an ocean liner,
its surrounding buildings
were constructed in
a variety of
architectural styles.
It was promoted as
America's first outdoor
shopping mall, now
it is an office complex.
Its neon-lit globe continues
to rotate to this day.

Opposite:
Sunset Towers, 1929.
Now the
Sunset Tower Hotel.
8358 Sunset Boulevard,
Los Angeles, CA, USA.
Architect:
Leland A. Bryant.

The former residential
building is decorated with
plaster frieze relief panels
of images of nude figures,
a Chinese pagoda,
a Zeppelin, plus
a squadron of aircraft.

Above:
Glazed tile buttress.
Eastern-Columbia Building,
1929.

This page and opposite:
Eastern-Columbia Building,
1929.
Now luxury apartments.
849 S. Broadway
and Ninth Street,
Los Angeles, CA, USA.
Architect:
Claude Beelman.

Right:
Turquoise and cerulean
blue terracotta with
accents of gold leaf,
facade,
four-sided clock tower,
Eastern-Columbia Building,
1929.

Opposite:
Building entrance,
Eastern-Columbia Building,
1929.

Established as a
clock company,
Eastern moved into
clothing when it purchased
the Columbia Outfitting
Company.

FOUNDED BY ADOLPH SIEROTY

Above:
Terazzo floor, lobby,
City of Santa Monica seal,
Santa Monica City Hall,
1939.

Right:
Facade,
Santa Monica City Hall,
1939.
1685 Main Street,
Santa Monica, CA, USA.
Architects:
Donald B. Parkinson
and Joseph Estep.

Tile decoration above
the entrance.
Santa Monica City Hall,
1939.
1685 Main Street,
Santa Monica, CA, USA.
Tiles produced by
The Gladding-McBean
Company.

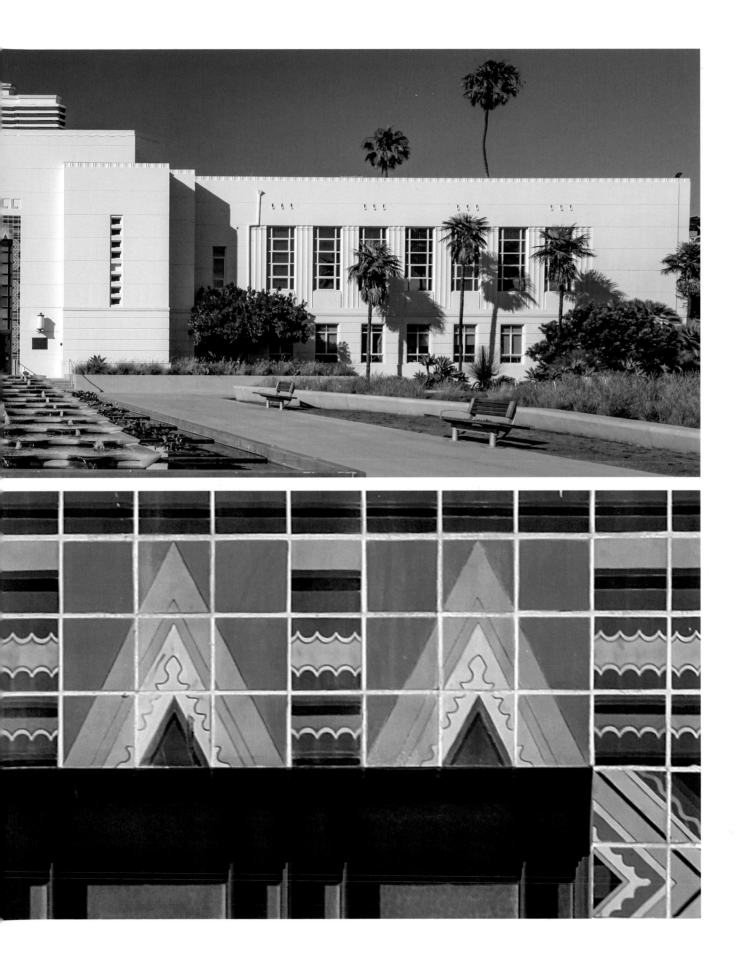

Detail,
punched metal frieze,
Grandstand rear facade,
Santa Anita Racetrack,
1937.
285 W. Huntington Drive,
Arcadia, CA, USA.
Architect:
Gordon B. Kaufmann.

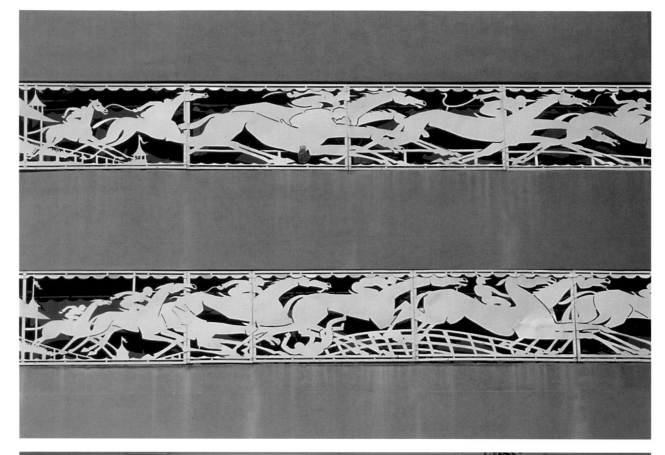

Clubhouse facade,
Santa Anita Racetrack,
1937.
285 W. Huntington Drive,
Arcadia, CA, USA.
Architect:
Gordon B. Kaufmann.

Detail,
metal entrance gate.
Valentine Elementary
School, 1937-38.
1650 Huntington Drive,
San Marino, CA, USA.
Architects:
Norman Marsh,
Donald Smith
and Herbert Powell.

"Kindergarten",
metal entrance gate.
Valentine Elementary
School, 1937-38.
1650 Huntington Drive,
San Marino, CA, USA.
Architects:
Norman Marsh,
Donald Smith
and Herbert Powell.

Above:
Glazed tile
drinking fountain,
Valentine Elementary
School, 1937–38.

147

Above:
Detail,
double bronze grille doors,
First Class restaurant,
RMS Queen Mary, 1934.
Artist: Walter Gilbert.

Right:
Planter/light fixture,
one of a pair originally
in the First Class
Dining Room, now in
the Main Hall and
Shopping Center
RMS Queen Mary, 1934.
Now a hotel
and tourist attraction.
1126 Queens Highway,
Long Beach, CA, USA.
Built by John Brown
and Company Ltd.

Far right:
Light fixture,
First Class Main Lounge,
RMS Queen Mary, 1934.

Below:
First Class swimming pool,
RMS Queen Mary, 1934.

During World War II,
the ship was used
as a troop carrier.
The pool was transformed
into sleeping quarters
for the troops.

It is said that the pool
is haunted, as two
passengers had
drowned there.

Carved gesso panel
"Unicorns in Battle"
above the main fireplace.
First Class Main Lounge.
RMS Queen Mary, 1934.
1126 Queens Highway,
Long Beach, CA, USA.
Artists:
Alfred J. Oakley and
Gilbert Bayes.

During World War Two,
the RMS Queen Mary
was known as the
"Grey Ghost", due to its
wartime camouflage.
It transported nearly
17,000 American troops
across the Atlantic.

The Architect and Building
News' 1936 review of
the new ship was
"Mild but expensive vulgarity".

Above:
"Cocktail Time" wall clock,
Observation Lounge
and Cocktail Bar.
RMS Queen Mary, 1934.

Right:
Decorative balustrade,
Observation Lounge
and Cocktail Bar.
RMS Queen Mary, 1934.
Now a hotel
and tourist attraction.
1126 Queens Highway,
Long Beach, CA, USA.
Artist:
Austin Crompton Roberts.

Woods from different parts
of the British Empire were
used in the ship's public
rooms and staterooms.

Detail, etched glass, balustrade, Verandah Grill and Cocktail Lounge. RMS Queen Mary, 1934.
Now a hotel and tourist attraction. 1126 Queens Highway, Long Beach, CA, USA.
Built by John Brown and Company Ltd.

Detail, "The Royal Jubilee Week 1935" mural.
Observation Lounge and Cocktail Bar, RMS Queen Mary, 1934.
1126 Queens Highway, Long Beach, CA, USA.
Artist: Alfred R. Thomson.

The mural over the Lounge Bar celebrates King George V's Silver Jubilee.

Above:
Metal grille,
box office,
Catalina Casino, 1927.

This page and opposite:
Murals depicting sea life,
Catalina Casino, 1927.
1 Catalina Way,
Avalon,
Catalina Island, CA, USA.
Architects:
Webber & Spaulding.
Artist:
John Gabriel Beckman.

Above:
Detail, bronze tryptich,
**this spread,
and following two spreads:**
Bronze relief panels
designed by
Thomas M. James.
State Street Trust Building,
1929.
75–101 Franklin Street,
Boston, MA, USA.
Architect:
Thomas M. James.

The bronze panel images
of sailors, aviators, farmers,
carpenter, stonemasons,
and blacksmiths represent
finance, architecture,
sculpture, agriculture,
power, and transportation.

Above:
Granite intaglio
decoration,
Suffolk County
Courthouse, 1937.

Right:
Metal grille, main entrance,
Suffolk County
Courthouse, 1937.
3 Pemberton Square,
Boston, MA, USA.
Architects:
Desmond & Lord.

"Justice for All",
granite sculptural figures
above the entrance.
Suffolk County
Courthouse, 1937,
3 Pemberton Square,
Boston, MA, USA.
Architects:
Desmond & Lord.

One of a number
of copper panels,
New England Power
building.
433–447 Stuart Street,
Boston, MA.
Architects:
Cram & Ferguson.

High Street entrance,
United Shoe Machinery
Corporation Building,
1928–30.
160 Federal Street,
Boston, MA, USA.
Architects:
Parker, Thomas & Rice,
with Henry Bailey Alden.

Above:
Detail,
gilded bell, symbol of the
New England Telephone
and Telegraph Company.

Right:
Detail,
United Shoe Machinery
Corporation Building,
1928–30.
160 Federal Street,
Boston, MA, USA.
Architects:
Parker, Thomas & Rice,
with Henry Bailey Alden.

Opposite:
New England Telephone
and Telegraph Company.
Post Office Square,
185 Franklin Street,
Boston, MA, USA.
Designed in 1939 and
completed in 1947.
Architects:
Cram & Ferguson.

Above:
Stone low relief
Crane sculpture,
Abbey House, 1940.
300 21st Street,
Miami Beach, FL, USA.
Architect:
Albert Anis.
Sculptor:
Robert Swartburg.

Right:
Beach Patrol
Headquarters, 1934.
1001 Ocean Drive,
Miami Beach, FL, USA.
Architect:
Robert A. Taylor.

Right, top:
Breakwater Hotel, 1939.
940 Ocean Drive,
Miami Beach, FL, USA.
Architect:
Anton Skislewicz.

Right, below:
Avalon Hotel, 1941.
700 Ocean Drive,
Miami Beach, FL, USA.
Architect:
Albert Anis.

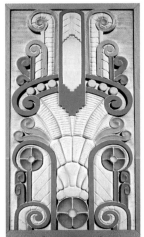

Above:
Plaster relief,
facade,
and left:
Congress Hotel, 1936.
1052 Ocean Drive,
Miami Beach, FL, USA.
Architect:
Henry Hohauser.

Crescent Hotel,
1932.
1420 Ocean Drive,
Miami Beach, FL, USA.
Architect:
Henry Hohauser.

Above:
Octagonal stone plaque,
Bentley Hotel, 1939.
Fifth Street,
and Ocean Drive,
Miami Beach, FL, USA.
Architect:
John Carlton Skinner.

Right:
Hotel Taft, 1936.
1040 Washington Avenue,
Miami Beach, FL, USA.
Architect:
Henry Hohauser.

Right:
Neon signage,
Kent Hotel, 1939.
1131 Collins Avenue,
Miami, FL, USA.
Architect:
L. Murray Dixon.

Far right:
The Palmer House,
1939.
1119 Collins Avenue,
Miami, FL, USA.
Architect:
L. Murray Dixon.

174

Above:
Chrome and glass
exterior light fitting,
The Savoy Hotel, 1935.
425 Ocean Drive,
Miami Beach, FL, USA.
Architect:
Albert Anis.

Left:
McAlpin Hotel, 1940.
1424 Ocean Drive,
Miami Beach, FL, USA.
Architect:
L. Murray Dixon.

Barbizon Hotel.
556 Ocean Drive,
Miami Beach, FL, USA.

Above:
Detail, relief,
Franklin Hotel, 1934.
860 Collins Avenue,
Miami Beach, FL, USA.
Architect:
V.H. Nellenbogen.

Right:
The Carlyle, 1941.
1250 Ocean Drive,
Miami Beach, FL, USA.
Architects:
Kiehnel & Elliott.

The Webster Hotel, 1939.
1220 Collins Avenue,
Miami Beach, FL, USA.
Architect:
Henry Hohauser.

Above:
Neon sign,
Edison Hotel, 1935.
960 Ocean Drive,
Miami, FL, USA.
Architect:
Henry Hohauser.

Left:
Colony Hotel, 1935.
736 Ocean Drive,
Miami, FL, USA.
Architect:
Henry Hohauser.

Above:
Etched glass window,
and right:
Tiffany Hotel, 1939.
801 Collins Avenue,
Miami Beach, FL, USA.
Architect:
L. Murray Dixon.

Essex House, 1938.
1001 Collins Avenue,
Miami Beach, FL, USA.
Architect:
Henry Hohauser.

Far left:
Essex House, 1938.
1001 Collins Avenue,
Miami Beach, FL, USA.
Architect:
Henry Hohauser.

Left:
Tiffany Hotel, 1939.
801 Collins Avenue,
Miami Beach, FL, USA.
Architect:
L. Murray Dixon.

Detail, silvered
wrought iron terrace railing,
Sherbrooke Hotel,
1947.

Left:
Sherbrooke Hotel,
1947.
901 Collins Avenue
Miami Beach, FL, USA.
Architect:
MacKay & Gibbs.

Above:
Detail, terrazzo
terrace floor,
and right:
Hotel Bancroft, 1939.
1501 Collins Avenue,
Miami Beach, FL, USA.
Architect:
Albert Anis.

Haddon Hall, 1941.
500 Collins Avenue,
Miami Beach, FL, USA.
Architect:
L. Murray Dixon.
Sculptor:
Robert M. Schwarz.

Above:
Detail,
decorative stone
shop facade,
Washington Boulevard,
Miami Beach, FL, USA.

Left:
Three Keystone
bas-reliefs,
Miami Beach
Public Library, 1930.
Now Bass Museum.
2100 Collins Avenue,
Miami Beach, FL, USA.
Architects:
Arata Isozaki,
Russel T. Pancoast.
Sculptor:
Gustav Bohland.

Above:
Detail,
stone relief sculpture,
Abbey House, 1940.
300 21st Street,
Miami Beach, FL, USA.
Architect:
Albert Anis.
Sculptor:
Robert Swartburg.

Top left:
Facade,
and below:
Interior tiled staircase,
The Parkway, 1936.
736 13th Street,
Miami Beach, FL, USA.
Architect:
Henry Hohauser.

Top right:
Seahorse railings,
residential complex.
Miami Beach, FL, USA.

Opposite:
Screen door,
private residence.
1015 Lenox Avenue,
Miami Beach, FL, USA.

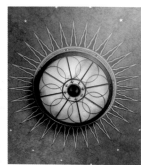

Above:
Detail,
rotunda ceiling design,
Miami Beach
Main Post Office, 1939.
Artist:
Charles Hardman.

Right:
Miami Beach
Main Post Office, 1939.
1300 Washington Avenue,
Miami Beach, FL, USA.
Architect:
Howard L. Cheney.

A WPA (Works Progress
Administration) project.

Above:
Etched glass window,
Hoffman's Cafeteria,
1939.

Right:
Hoffman's Cafeteria, 1939.
Later Jerry's Famous Deli.
Now Señor Frogs.
1450 Collins Avenue,
Miami Beach, FL, USA.
Architect:
Henry Hohauser.

Victor Hotel, 1937.
1144 Ocean Drive,
Miami Beach, FL, USA.
Architect:
L. Murray Dixon.

Above:
Wall inset light fitting,
Victor Hotel, 1937.

Right:
Light fittings and mural,
lobby,
Victor Hotel, 1937.
1144 Ocean Drive,
Miami Beach, FL, USA.
Architect: L. Murray Dixon.
Muralist: Earl La Pan.

Mural,
Plymouth Hotel, 1940.
336 21st Street,
Miami Beach, FL, USA.
Architect:
Anton Skislewicz.

Above:
Friedman's Bakery,
1930s.
Now Manolo Restaurant.
685 Washington Avenue.
Miami Beach, FL, USA

Right:
Facade,
Surf Hotel, 1936.
Now a restaurant.
444 Ocean Drive,
Miami Beach, FL, USA.
Architect:
Henry Hohauser.

Fish and seaweed
decoration,
Marlin Hotel, 1939.
1200 Collins Avenue,
Miami Beach, FL, USA.
Architect: L. Murray Dixon.

Above:
Detail,
and right:
Facade,
Mayfair Hotel, 1936.
1960 Park Avenue,
Miami Beach, FL, USA.
Architect:
Henry Hohauser.

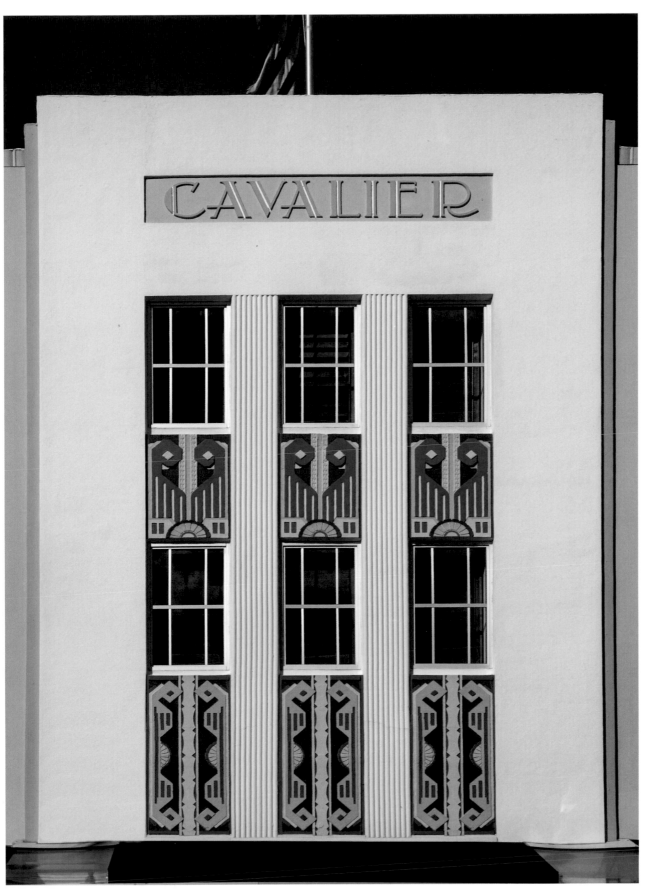

Facade,
Cavalier Hotel, 1936.
1320 Ocean Drive,
Miami Beach, FL, USA.
Architect:
Roy F. France.

Above:
Glass blocks box office;
Cameo Theatre, 1938.

This page and opposite:
Fluted columns and
glass blocks facade.
Cameo Theatre, 1938.
1445 Washington Avenue,
Miami Beach, FL, USA.
Architect:
Robert E. Collins.

Keystone relief
decorative flourishes
frame a cameo portrait,
Cameo Theatre, 1938.

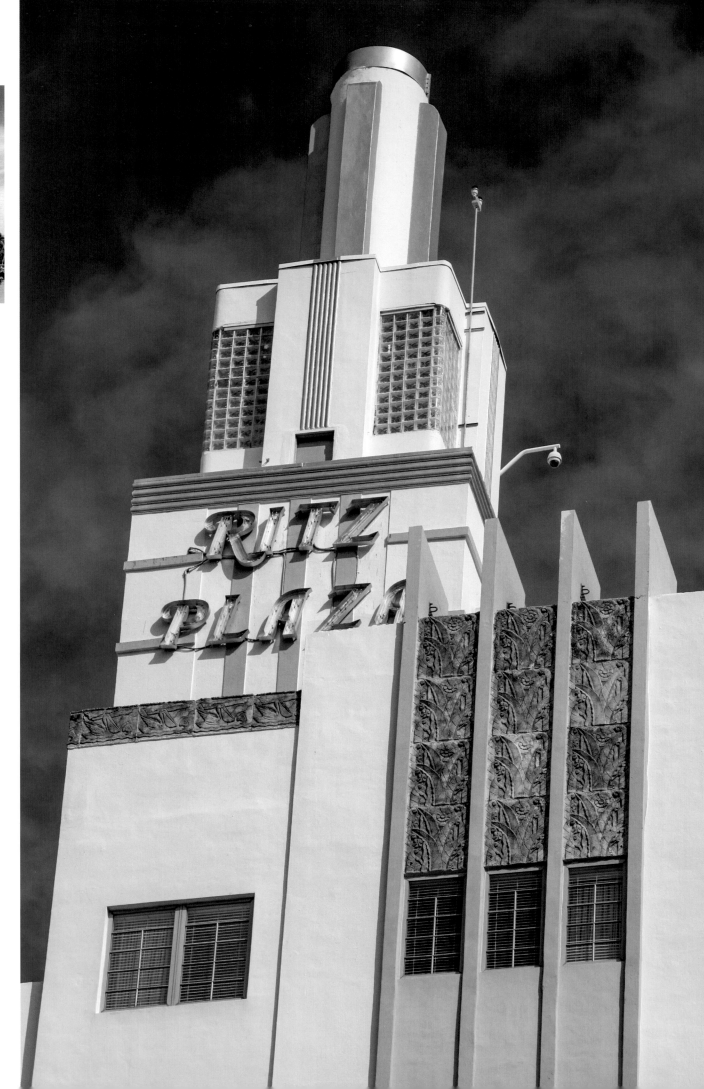

Dimensional signage,
Shelborne Hotel, 1940.
1801 Collins Avenue,
Miami Beach, FL, USA.
Architect:
Igor B. Polevitsky.

National Hotel, 1940.
1677 Collins Avenue,
Miami Beach, FL, USA.
Architect:
Roy F. France.

Above:
Detail, Delano Hotel,
1685 Collins Avenue,
Miami Beach, FL, USA.

Right:
Sagamore Hotel, 1943.
1631 Collins Avenue,
Miami Beach, FL, USA.
Architect: Albert Anis.

Opposite:
St Moritz, 1939.
1565 Collins Avenue,
Miami Beach, FL, USA.
Architect:
Roy F. France.

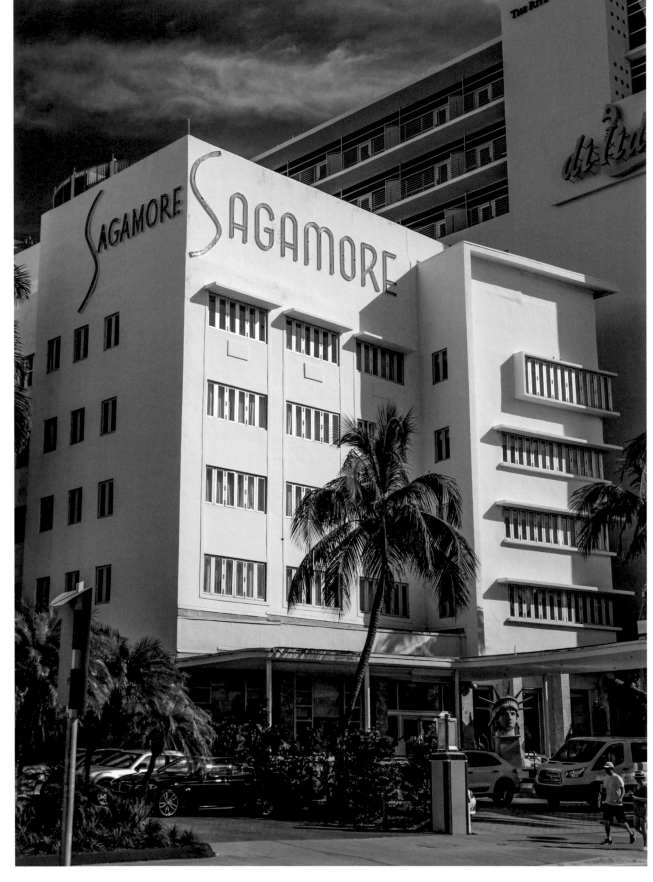

This page and opposite:
Empire State Building,
1930–1949.
350 Fifth Avenue,
New York, NY. USA.
Architects:
Shreve, Lamb
and Harmon.

The spire was originally
constructed as a
mooring mast for airships.
The building was
immortalized in the film
"King Kong", 1933.

Right:
Gilded panel,
above the front desk, lobby,
Empire State Building,
1930–1949.

Opposite:
Tower,
Empire State Building,
1930–1949.

Above:
Brass on marble signage,
The Chanin Building, 1932.

Right:
Terracotta facade,
The Chanin Building, 1932.
122 East 42nd Street
and Lexington Avenue,
New York, NY, USA.
Architect:
Jacques L. Delamarre.
Sculptor:
Rene Chambellan.

Polychrome
bas-relief sculpture,
"Progress",
Rockefeller Center, 1937.
49th Street entrance,
New York, NY, USA.
Sculptor: Lee Lawrie.

Gilded sculpture,
"Prometheus",
Rockefeller Center, 1937.
45 Rockefeller Plaza,
Fifth Avenue,
New York, NY, USA.
Sculptor:
Paul Manship.

Located on the
Lower Plaza.
The quote carved in the
red granite wall behind
the sculpture is taken from
the sixth-century B.C.
Greek dramatist Aeschylus:
"Prometheus, Teacher in
Every Art, Brought the Fire
That Hath Proved
to Mortals a Means to
Mighty Ends".

Above:
"Genius seizing the Light of the Sun", one of four stone carvings, "Aspect of Mankind". Rockefeller Plaza, 1250 Avenue of the Americas, New York, NY, USA. Sculptor: Gaston Lachasie.

Left:
Facade, entrance to the International Building, Rockefeller Center, 1937. 45 Rockefeller Plaza, Fifth Avenue, New York, NY, USA. Architect: Raymond Hood. Sculptor: Lee Lawrie.

"Winged Mercury,"
intaglio relief.
Rockefeller Center, 1937.
620 Fifth Avenue entrance,
New York, NY, USA.
Sculptor: Lee Lawrie.

"Light", 1937,
facade,
Rockefeller Center,
30 Rockefeller Plaza,
Fifth Avenue,
New York, NY, USA.
Sculptor: Lee Lawrie.
Polychrome painting:
Leon V. Solon.

The sculptures
"Sound" and "Light"
flank "Wisdom".

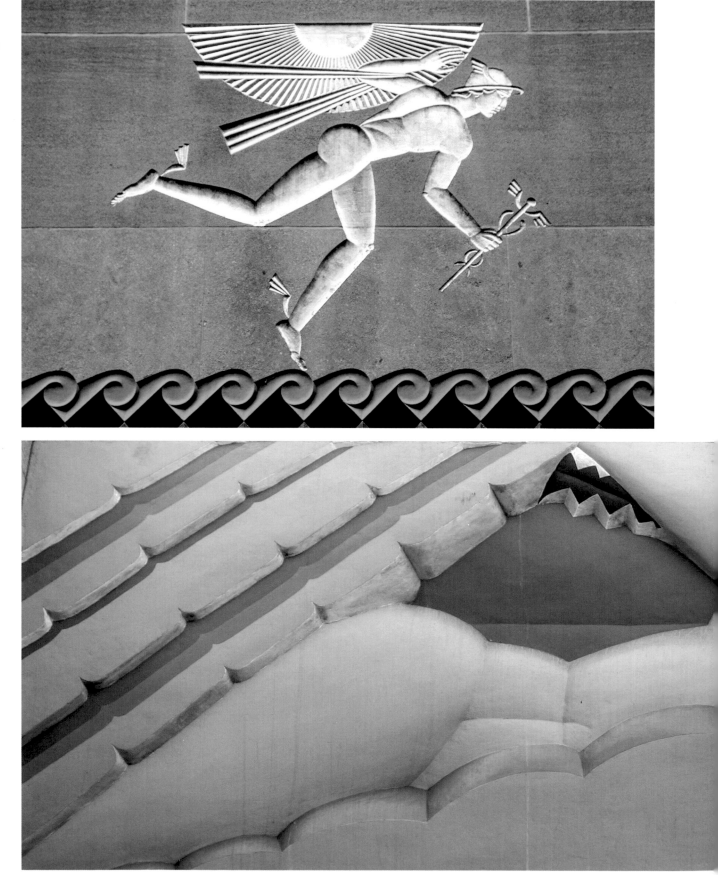

"Seeds of Good
Citizenship,"
intaglio relief,
Rockefeller Center, 1937.
610 Fifth Avenue,
New York, NY, USA.
Sculptor: Lee Lawrie.

Located at the entrance
to La Maison Francaise.

Above:
"Sound,"
facade,
Rockefeller Center, 1937.
Sculptor:
Lee Lawrie.

This page and opposite:
Enameled brass roundels,
south facade,
Radio City Music Hall,
1932.
Sixth Avenue and
West 50th Street,
New York, NY, USA.
Architect:
Edward Durrell Stone.
Artist:
Hildreth Meière.
Design executed by
Oscar Bach.

Top right:
"Song".

Below:
"Dance".

Opposite:
"Drama".

The three 18-ft diameter
plaques on the
West 50th Street facade
are made of
chromium steel,
duraluminium,
bronze, nickel-bronze,
copper and brass.

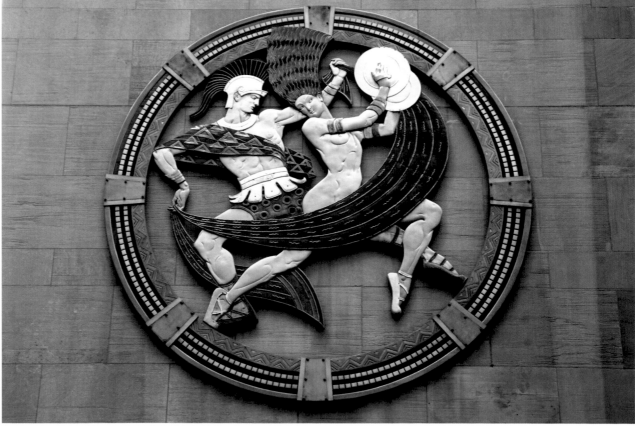

Above:
Stone relief medallion,
Federal Building, 1935.
90 Church Street,
New York, NY, USA.
Architects:
Cross & Cross
(with Pennington,
Lewis & Mills.
Sculptor:
Carl Paul Jennewein.

Brass pavement
street sign.
Rockefeller Plaza,
636 Fifth Avenue,
New York, NY, USA.

This page and opposite:
Five of six
cast bronze plaques
on granite
representing
"Acts from Vaudeville".
Facade,
Radio City Music Hall,
1932.
1260 Sixth Avenue,
New York, NY, USA.
Sculptor:
Rene Paul Chambellan.

Above:
Detail, gold-leaf relief
on granite, facade,
Waldorf Astoria Hotel, 1931.
301 Park Avenue,
New York, NY, USA.
Architects:
Schultze & Weaver.

Right:
Pediment,
The Fuller Construction
Company Building, 1929.
East 57th Street,
New York, NY, USA.
Architects:
Walker and Gillette.
Sculptor: Elie Nadelman.

BUILDING

Above:
One of several
colored bas-reliefs of
workers and artisans,
Green Building, 1928.
100 Sixth Avenue
and Watts Street,
New York, NY, USA.
Architect:
Ely Jacques Kahn.

This page and opposite:
Bas-relief figures
on the west facade.
Graybar Building, 1927.
420 Lexington Avenue,
New York, NY, USA.
Architects:
Sloan and Robertson.

The building was named
for the first tenant,
Graybar Electric Company.

Above:
Brass signage,
42nd Street exit,
the Chrysler Building,
1928–1930.

Right:
Entrance,
the Chrysler Building,
1928–1930.
405 Lexington Avenue,
New York, NY, USA.
Architect:
William Van Alen.

Opposite:
Silver and grey
Nircosta metal spire,
the Chrysler Building,
1928–1930.
405 Lexington Avenue,
New York, NY, USA.
Architect:
William Van Alen.

Do you or don't you?
That is the question.
Some do. Some don't.
Some think it's a freak; some
think it's a stunt.
A few think it is positively
ugly; others consider it
a great feat, a masterpiece,
a "tour de force".
— The American Architect.

Above:
Sculpted eagle
exterior light fitting,
Department of
Health, Hospital and
Sanitation Building, 1930s.
New York, NY, USA.
Sculptor: Oscar Bach.

Right, above:
The Airlines Terminal, 1939.
Demolished in 1978.
80 East 42nd Street,
New York, NY, USA.
Architect: John B. Peterkin.

A 1941 New York Times
article described the
interiors of the Terminal
as being equipped with
"modern mechanisms" that
gave it an "Arabian Nights
atmosphere".

Right, below:
Detail, ceiling mural,
"Energy, Result,
Workmanship,
and Transportation",
the Chrysler Building,
1928-1930.
405 Lexicon Avenue,
New York, NY, USA.
Architect:
William Van Alen.
Muralist: Edward Turnbull.

Detail shows
Charles Lindbergh flying
The Spirit of St. Louis
across the Atlantic.
It was the largest mural
in the world.

Opposite:
Granite facade,
The News Building, 1930.
220 East 42nd St,
New York, NY, USA.
Architects:
John Mead Howells
and Raymond Hood.

Above:
Detail, glazed tiles,
facade,
Gramercy House, 1930.
235 East 22nd Street,
New York, NY, USA.
Architects:
George and Edward Blum.

Right:
Glazed tiled facade,
Art Deco Egyptian
Revival style,
Knights of Pythias
Building, 1927.
Now a condominium.
135 West 70th Street,
New York, NY, USA.
Architect:
Thomas W. Lamb.

A further example of
Egyptian Revival
architecture, inspired
by Howard Carter's
1920 discovery of
Tutankham's Tomb.
In the 1940s, the building
was taken over by
Decca Records.
Among the many artists
who recorded there are
Bill Hailey and his Comets
("Rock Around the Clock").

Opposite:
Detail, bronze bust,
The Brill Building, 1930-31.
1619 Broadway,
New York, NY, USA.
Architect:
Victor A. Bark, Jr.

The bust is of the
building's developer
Abraham Lefcourt's son,
Alan, who died of anemia
aged 17.

Two silvered
bas-relief plaques,
facade,
NYC Department of
Health, Hospital and
Sanitation Building,
1932–1935.
125 Worth Street,
New York, NY, USA.
Architect:
Charles B. Meyers.
Sculptor: Oscar Bach.

Above:
Detail,
Madison Belmont Building,
1924–25,
40 East 34th Street,
New York, NY, USA.
Architects:
Warren & Westmore.
Ironwork:
Edgar Brandt.

Right:
Wrought-iron door grilles,
Numbers 5 and 8.
Gracie Square,
New York, NY, USA.

Opposite:
"Fountain" decoration,
facade,
Essex House.
160 Central Park South,
New York, NY, USA.

Above:
US Postal Service
stamp, 2003.

Right:
"Wisdom" sculpture,
façade,
Rockefeller Center, 1937.
30 Rockefeller Plaza,
Fifth Avenue,
New York, NY, USA.
Sculptor: Lee Lawrie.